You can return this item to any library but please
note that not all libraries are open every day.
Items must be returned on or before the due date.
Failure to do so will result in overdue charges.
Items may be renewed unless requested by
another customer, in person or by telephone, on
two occasions only. Your membership card number
will be required.
Please look after this item – you may be charged
for any damage.

Headquarters:
Information, Culture & Community Learning,
Town Hall, Bournemouth BH2 6DY

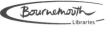

For further success in all aspects of business, be sure to read these other businesspartners books:

Successful Coaching & Mentoring
Successful Project Management
Successful Time Management

businesspartners

successful
interviews

Ken Lawson, M.A., Ed.M.

This edition first published in 2009 by New Holland Publishers (UK) Ltd
London • Cape Town • Sydney • Auckland
www.newhollandpublishers.com

Garfield House, 86–88 Edgware Road, London W2 2EA, United Kingdom
80 McKenzie Street, Cape Town 8001, South Africa
Unit 1, 66 Gibbes Street, Chatswood, NSW 2067, Australia
218 Lake Road, Northcote, Auckland, New Zealand

10 8 6 4 2 1 3 5 7 9

© 2005 Axis Publishing Limited
8c Accommodation Road
London NW11 8ED
www.axispublishing.co.uk

NOTE: The opinions and advice expressed in this book are intended as a guide only. The publisher
and author accept no responsibility for any loss sustained as a result of using this book.

ISBN: 978-1-84773-397-9

Printed and bound in Korea

contents

Introduction

The thought of being interviewed for a new position is usually accompanied by a choking sense of fear and dread. What if I can't answer the questions intelligently? What if my interviewer is intimidating? What if I don't describe my strengths persuasively? What if my mind goes blank and I cannot formulate the answers to even the simplest questions? In short – what if I fail?

It's true that the job interview, in whatever form it may take, is one of the most stressful events in the business world. But it's one that you shouldn't avoid, no matter how stressful, because interviews are necessary for career advancement and success. The only individuals who don't have to confront the prospect of the job interview are those whose careers are going nowhere: you're not one of them.

So, how do you turn this dreaded event into a rich opportunity for career success? The answer lies in anticipating the interview environment and taking control of as many aspects of the interview process as possible. And that involves a creative recipe of systematic self-assessment, research and preparation, all seasoned with a generous helping of informed intuition. If you can achieve the right blend of these ingredients and allow them to shape the mindset with which you come to the interview, you're doing everything you can to tip the outcome in your favour.

Successful Interviews will show you how to make the interview work in your favour and will strengthen your application when you make your next career move. Whether you're still in the early stages of your career or hold a more senior position, this book gives you the tools, tips and guidelines you will need to make the most of the momentous career opportunity that the interview presents.

You'll learn how to be methodical and thorough in your preparation, including how to research the company interviewing you and its position within the marketplace. Then you'll take stock of your unique portfolio of professional qualities and experience and learn how to express them fluently using the type of persuasive language that will sound convincing on the day of the interview.

A comprehensive chapter on interview behaviours and dynamics provides detailed advice to help you anticipate and master the many facets of this unique human interaction. You'll learn about the various types of interviews and how to respond to each of them. This book will serve as your personal career coach throughout the process, offering step-by-step techniques to help you meet and conquer the interview challenge with confidence and flair.

A huge amount of the stress attached to the prospect of interviewing is triggered by ambiguity and fear of the unknown. *Successful Interviews* will help you banish those dreadful sensations and allow you to focus your energy on the critical component in every interview situation – YOU.

Ultimately, it's your unique blend of attributes and experience that will get you the position you covet. *Successful Interviews* will help you showcase your qualifications for the job, unlocking your potential for continued personal career success, as well as highlighting how you can enhance your future organization. Your decision to read and absorb this book might best be described as a brilliant career move.

Ken Lawson, M.A., Ed.M.
Career management counsellor and author
Instructor, School of Continuing and Professional Studies
New York University

1

researching the company

Why do company research?

There are many good reasons why you should do some thorough research on the company that has invited you for an interview.

1 IT DEMONSTRATES YOUR COMMITMENT TO GETTING THE JOB
Chances are, if you have done it thoroughly, this research has taken up a considerable amount of your 'me' time. This shows that you are serious about your application and interest in the company.

2 YOU WILL BE BETTER INFORMED THAN THE OTHER CANDIDATES
Remember that all the candidates invited for an interview can probably do the job; what you want to do is to prove that you will do it best. A good understanding of the company's work and profile can help you in this.

3 YOU HAVE SHOWN INITIATIVE
The research you have done – and the different types of research you have done – will demonstrate your intelligence and tenacity.

4 YOU WILL UNDERSTAND THE NEED TO FILL THE POSITION
The more you find out about the company, the greater
understanding you will have about why this position is
important at this time and what you need to emphasize
about your qualifications to fill the vacancy.

5 IT MIGHT MAKE YOU THINK TWICE ABOUT PROCEEDING
A company report, for example, might talk about regrouping or
retrenchment next year; do you want to be in HR (Human
Resources) to make staff redundant? Is this position likely to
be part of any downsizing? Alternatively, it might talk about
relocating core services: Is this a good time for you to relocate?

Organizational life cycles

All companies go through similar life cycles. Establishing where your potential employer is in the life cycle can help you to focus your research and decide whether this is really where you want to be.

STARTUP

This is fairly obviously a new company. The demise of so many Internet startup companies meant that startup companies got a poor reputation, but there are lots of advantages of being involved with a company at the beginning and sharing in its development and success.

GROWTH

A successful startup company then moves into a period of growth. Most people who start companies have an optimum size or product range in mind from the beginning, although this might evolve, with success. For example, many companies are limited initially by their capitalization. A small advertising company could not afford to pitch for the account of a global presence. Alternatively, a company's philosophy could be to make everything by hand, which might limit output to a relatively small number of units annually. Success tends to solve or alleviate capitalization issues and a company might continue to grow.

RETRENCHMENT

A company hits a wall. The market for a product or service declines, or someone else introduces something new and a company's profitability starts to fall. A good business analyst might be able to suggest ways to 'sit it out', for example, by outsourcing some services or regrouping some divisions, but usually there are really only two possible outcomes here: diversification or decline.

DIVERSIFICATION

Altering a core activity in response to either market need or technological innovation is sound business sense. For example, a few years ago any company whose core business was making films might have diversified into making digital-processing equipment. Several major telephone handset manufacturers diversified into mobile phone manufacture and so on. Successful diversification may mean that a company goes back to startup or growth status.

DECLINE

Too little diversification too late means an organization goes into decline. This can be rapid or more drawn out. Handling decline is a career option in itself: outsourcing workers successfully, selling or decommissioning buildings and winding up accounts all take skill and sensitivity.

LIFE CYCLES AND YOU

Identifying where a company is in its life cycle can help you to decide whether this is a good match for you. If you are young, energetic and enthusiastic, you might take a chance on a startup company and who cares if you work all night, you're building a great team and a great profile. If you have family responsibilities, you might prefer the relative security of a company that is growing or diversifying. And if you are an ideas person, spotting a company's potential to diversify at just the right time could mean that you are one day running the company.

Company website

It sounds obvious, but one of the easiest and most accessible ways to learn about a company is from its website. Not only does this tell you how user-friendly the organization is, but it also gives a real insight into how they see themselves in the marketplace. Look at the following specific areas.

MARKET POSITION

'We have offices in 17 countries on three continents' is completely different from 'We are the largest retailers of X products in Brighton, England, or Perth, Australia'. You need to know whether you are applying to a leading local company, a multinational or anything in between. This information can help you formulate questions and pinpoint the direction in which the organization is going.

WHO'S WHO

A major player will list its CEO, directors and other chief officers. with their areas of expertise and interest. You might also find keynote speeches they have made recently, together with press releases. This can give you an insight into company dynamics: How many CEOs are women? How many directors are middle-aged men? How many of the most important people are from academic or technical backgrounds? This is all useful information that will help you assess your 'fit' within the company.

VACANCIES

There may well be a page of positions that need filling, including the one in which you are interested. Check how many there are in relation to the size of the organization. Is this indicative of high turnover or does it simply mean the organization is expanding rapidly? Can you see a future in more than one area of the company?

PRODUCTS AND SERVICES

You may be surprised at the range of company products or services, but a good understanding of what all areas of the company are involved with can only help you at the interview. See if there is an area devoted to 'new releases' or 'coming soon' so that you can ask about it at your interview and demonstrate that you have a good knowledge of, and interest in, everything the company is currently marketing.

COMPANY REPORT/SHAREHOLDER INFORMATION

It will save you further research (see pp. 22–23) if this type of information is on the website. The multinationals tend to include it; smaller companies may not. This could give you a good handle on turnover, profitability, year-on-year growth and other issues that might be important in deciding if this is the right company for you.

PRESS CONTACTS

If there is a link for the media, use it to ask questions that you have not been able to answer elsewhere on the site. For example, 'How many people are employed at your facility at X?', 'When will the CXP10 be available in stores?' or 'When can I buy directly from you?'

This is likely to be the area where most of the news or breaking news stories can be found.

ETHICS

There may be a statement on company ethics, especially with larger companies, or those that tend to have an (often misplaced) poor media profile. For example, oil companies will position themselves in the best possible environmental light. More local companies might point out what they do for the community.

Such statements show a company's commitment to more than simply making a profit for its shareholders.

EMPLOYEE EVENTS

There might be images of a Summer Picnic or a Christmas Party. This sort of information tells you that employees and families are important. It also gives you an insight into how the company works: an invite to a black tie event just for couples sends out a completely different signal than a family evening event, for example.

It may be that the company does not have employee events, so if your social life has been based around your colleagues, it is worth knowing this early on.

researching the company

Company report

A company's annual report to its shareholders is a good source of information for you. A report will give information on such factors as the following:

KEY ACHIEVEMENTS OF THE PAST YEAR
This might be something like 'Achieved profitability in all sectors' or 'Successfully opened new facility in Europe'.

MARKET SHARE AND SECTOR SHARE
For example, how the company performed against its rivals (e.g., 'We now have 20 percent of the global market, as opposed to our closest rival who has 8 percent'). This should also tell you the internal market shares, for example, 'Photocopiers continue to be our core business, generating 20 percent of our operating profit, but digital cameras are now generating 15 percent of our profit and this is still rising'. This section may also indicate profits by territory.

PROFITABILITY OF DIFFERENT GROUPS
Larger companies are umbrellas for several smaller, focused groups. The relative strengths and profitability of these smaller groups will probably be addressed. This might help you see that the sector you are considering joining might be small, but it is returning good profits, for example, or that although you want to join the biggest manufacturing area or core business, this is less profitable than other divisions of the business.

NEW PRODUCTS AND SERVICES
You will find from this section what has been introduced, what is up-and-coming or forthcoming and whether there is a real commitment to research and development.

STRATEGY
The company's plans for the coming year and possibly longer, will be included as shareholders want to know what their money is being spent on, and what the likely return will be.

There are two areas where you might want to look for additional information. Failing to find it is not necessarily a cause for concern, but seeing the below sends the right signals:

- The first is anything along the lines of 'investment in people' or 'training and development'; that is, that this company values its workers and actively supports training.

- The second area is something of a worldview; that is, that the company takes its environmental or humanitarian responsibilities seriously.

Press cuttings

It is a good idea to keep a file of press cuttings on companies you have targeted as being a good fit for you. In reality, many people do not and you might have to start from zero to get a dossier of recent press material together. There are some quick and easy ways to do this.

INTERNET

The Internet is a great timesaver if you are interested in a local, national or international company. Log into a search engine, type in the company name and near the top of the listing which comes up, you will find a news listing and an indication of when the story was posted. Alternatively, go to the company site and look for news stories there. Typle in the names of important people in the organization: You may get keynote speeches, academic papers, books and articles and other company-related information.

LIBRARY

For more local companies, try a library. The ease and speed of this reference source depends on how records are stored, but it should not take too long to find news stories on local companies.
Look in back issues of town and regional newspapers for relevant stories. If you do not have Internet access at home, you will almost certainly be able to log on at your local library.

TV AND RADIO STATIONS

Regional stations may have investigated and produced a story on a local company, even if nothing was actually aired. Call and speak to someone in the press office to see if you have missed anything recently. Keep in mind that a story may not have aired because it was unsubstantiated.

In all your research, remember to try and see the big picture (see pp. 36–37). A rival company shedding employees, a new superstore opening nearby, a new transport link or a merger between two of the industry's major players could all have an effect on the company in which you are interested.

researching the company

The line manager

Your best choice for information on the position is the line manager responsible for it; the name of the individual may have been included in the job advertisment. If not, you may have to do some creative detective work. His or her concern will be getting the right person for the position. So, make contact.

KEY QUESTIONS

1 Ask if the manager can send you any more literature on the company you are researching.

2 Call and ask to book a convenient time for an informal conversation (if appropriate).

3 Ask if a personal visit to the office can be arranged.

IF A TELEPHONE CONVERSATION IS ALL THAT IS POSSIBLE, THESE ARE THE AREAS THAT YOU SHOULD AIM TO COVER:

1 Is this a new position? If not:

2 How has this vacancy arisen (that is, what has happened to the person currently employed in the role)?

3 If the vacancy has arisen due to a promotion, can you speak to the person who was doing the job before (see pp. 30–31)?

KEY QUESTIONS

4 If it is a new position, how has it arisen (e.g. rapid expansion or a need for four financial controllers rather than three)?

5 Is there someone doing a similar job in another department, or another office in another city. Is it appropriate for you to talk to him or her?

6 Is this an immediate and real vacancy (or is the company seeing who is out there, without being committed to hiring anyone at this time)?

THE HUMAN RESOURCES DEPARTMENT

It is unlikely that human resources (HR) will have time to answer any questions about the position, although in most public or government service organizations there may be additional standard information that can be made available to any candidate. This is because HR departments are there to make sure that all applicants are treated fairly, and according to the law, and feel part of the wider corporate community. In this respect, HR staff are working for the benefit of everyone.

The most likely point of interaction with the HR department is likely to be at the formal interview.

The current holder of the position

Some organizations encourage applicants to talk informally with the person currently doing the job on offer, before putting in an application. If you did not, call and ask if it is still appropriate to talk for a few minutes 'off the record'.

The success of any discussion with the person currently doing the job depends on the reasons they are leaving it.

PROMOTION WITHIN THE ORGANIZATION
This is a good reason to be leaving because it tells you that the company promotes on merit, values staff retention, can spot potential and values career development.

MOVING TO ANOTHER DEPARTMENT

This reason is still positive. Either the person has done a good job and his or her skills are needed elsewhere, or there was a mismatch for this position and the person's skills are more relevant to other areas. This is another possible scenario that can be positive for someone coming in: the company can admit to making a mistake and will do something about it.

TRANSFER TO ANOTHER OFFICE IN ANOTHER CITY

This reason too indicates a commitment to staff retention and could point to the company's 'compassionate grounds' policy (were there family reasons for requesting and getting the move?). It could also say 'This person has done a great job here and is going elsewhere to improve standards there'.

Other employees

Ideally, you want to talk to people who are currently working in the organization you are hoping to join. Call and ask if this is appropriate and be candid about what you intend to ask. Areas that you might consider include:

COMPANY ETHOS

'I get the impression from all I've read that CP Holdings is a close-knit, family-friendly company. Would you say that was an accurate reflection?'

This might elicit a response such as 'Yes, that is broadly true, and certainly we place high stock on our employees feeling part of a team and working closely together. But that makes it doubly important that everyone contributes as much as they can'.

MESSAGE:

There is no place here for freeloaders, no matter how relaxed we seem.

RESULTS

'Your company report emphasized the year-on-year growth XY Advertising has achieved over the past five years. Is attracting new clients more important than other areas of the business?'

A response might be: 'We are committed to delivering creatively to all our clients, and client retention is important. However, this is a crowded market and attracting new clients is vital to our continuing growth'.

MESSAGE:

Every area of the business has to work together to maximum effect to keep the company successful.

PRESS
'There was a lot of adverse publicity
for this company over the
"Trailgate" affair. Would you say
that damaged company morale?'

A possible response: 'On the
contrary. We were all very much
behind the CEO when he went on
television to explain that we had
done nothing wrong – as indeed
the inquiry proved'.

MESSAGE:

We have a strong team here
and expect loyalty.

Friends and colleagues

Every job and every organization is unique, but if you ask around among your friends and colleagues, chances are you will find you know someone who knows someone who is either in a position similar to the one for which you've applied, or who is working in a similarly sized and positioned company. For example:

You have spent your whole career so far in small insurance companies and now you want to join a company with a global reputation. You don't need another insurance pro to talk to, you need someone who can give you information on what it's like to have to consider the world picture when making daily business decisions. The friend of a friend who works for a multinational copier company, bank or car manufacturer could give you this perspective.

You have been CEO of a manufacturing company and lost your position in a merger. Charity work appeals to you, but you are ignorant of this sector other than as a donor. Talk to anyone who has ever worked with a charity. The single biggest pitfall in work of this kind is that you are dealing with a lot of people who are not being paid and that is an alien concept to most managers to begin with. The second pitfall is the way that the tax department treats charities as opposed to businesses. If you can get your head around these issues by talking with an acquaintance, your other skills and experience will carry you a long way.

Getting the job would mean relocating and you are not sure if the company location is right for you. Your circle almost certainly includes someone who:

■ Was born in that particular area

■ Went to a local college or university

■ Worked for a company located near to the one for which you are considering working

■ Has a friend who works in that city

■ Has a friend who works for a rival company

Think laterally, and you will find you know where to go for a little inside information that is not compromising anyone else's integrity. This sort of networking is also how a lot of people move up the career ladder (see pp. 224–225) so take advantage of it at every opportunity.

Researching the marketplace

Hand in hand with your company research should go market research. This is important, whether you are moving from one company to another within the same industry or are applying for a similar job in a completely different type of company. You may think you keep abreast of industry

1 CURRENT TRENDS
- Are companies downsizing?

- Are they upscaling?

- Has a big player in the industry gone to the wall lately?

- How are the small companies doing?

2 FUTURE PROSPECTS
Are a lot of companies in your area in a similar phase of the organizational life cycle (see pp. 14–17)? If there has been a lot of startup activity lately, some of those companies are not likely to succeed. Can you tell which ones?

literature, but even the most motivated people miss out when they hit a busy period. Points 1 to 4 below are the factors that you should be looking out for to demonstrate at the interview a good understanding of the current market.

3 DEMAND AND INNOVATION
Technology is moving fast. Think logically about products, technologies, and industries that are going to adapt or become obsolete.

4 DEMOGRAPHICS
Some industries attract talent and keep it; others like a turnover to keep bringing in new blood. Look at other companies: How many CEOs in your business are over 50?

At the other end of the spectrum, how many are 'thirty-somethings' and what is the gender mix?

How many middle managers are just waiting for retirement and being allowed to do so?

Checklist: your research

When you think you have pulled all your research information together,
use this checklist:

1 Visited website and familiar with contents ☐

2 Read and understood company report ☐

3 Reviewed and understood financial profile ☐

4 Read press cuttings ☐

5 Researched marketplace ☐

6 Arranged company visit ☐

7 Talked with line manager ☐

8 Talked with other employees ☐

9 Talked with current employee in position ☐

2

who are you and
what are you selling?

Who will be interviewing me?

The interview process can give you information about the company and about the position. It will also add to the knowledge you are building up of how the company views the position for which you have applied.

If the interview is scheduled for late afternoon with only one executive, for example, it may send out the message that the position is not really regarded as that important.

Alternatively, if the interview is spread over two days and involves a number of one-on-one meetings, a presentation, and some form of social contact with future colleagues, you may begin to get a feel for the organization's level of commitment to the position to be filled.

When you are invited to be interviewed, find out:

■ Who will be interviewing you

■ Their positions in the company

This serves the purposes listed on the opposite page.

1 It establishes the company's view of the position.

2 It means that you won't attend an interview expecting to talk to one person and finding yourself speaking with four.

3 It gives you people to research, so that when you get into the room you can quickly match the faces to the names of the people interviewing you.

who are you and what are you selling?

Your profile

You need to show a potential employer the benefits that you will bring to the company or organization.

1 The effect you will have on the company's bottom line.

2 How much you will add to the profitability or turnover of the company.

3 The benefits (professional and personal) you will bring to the organization.

Your pitch may make the difference between success and being rejected. It should focus on your achievements. Focusing on your professional and personal attributes and your career to date will help you focus on the positive points you want to get across at the interview.

1 Analyze and include your key skills and key achievements to date and their outcomes.

2 Measure these against the information on the position you have gained from your research into the company.

3 Clearly establish in your own mind your personal attributes and how you will set these out and demonstrate them during the interview.

By analyzing your profile and linking your qualifications to the requirements for the open position, you can demonstrate why your career path makes you the right candidate.

who are you and what are you selling?

The job profile and you

In larger organizations, most jobs have fairly specific profiles, and candidates who do not meet most of the requirements are unlikely to be invited for an interview. If you received a profile as part of an application 'pack', you can work through it and check that you meet or exceed the requirements.

If there is not a formal profile, you are going to have to 'second guess' what the interviewer is looking for.

■ Look around your current company and check whether a job description exists for a position that is similar to the one for which you have applied.

■ Ask friends and colleagues in similar businesses whether they have a formal job description and whether you can see it.

Generally a job profile is broken down into a number of headings that you will need to study and understand so that you can match your skills, personality and experience to the position.

The headings are likely to be split between 'essentials' and 'desirables'. By reviewing the essentials, you may also be able to see how to develop your pitch at the interview and tailor it to meet the organization's needs.

THE HEADINGS WILL COVER THE FOLLOWING AREAS:

1 TECHNICAL
What you will be expected to be able to do.

2 EXPERIENCE
The position may call for a level of previous experience or a number of years in a particular industry or area of work.

3 SKILLS
The individual talents that are required for the position.

4 PERSONAL
The type of individual that the company requires which might be further divided into education, health, and other factors.

5 EDUCATION
This is the level of qualifications required.

6 HEALTH
This is likely to be along the lines of 'good general health' but may be more specific depending on the industry you work in. There may well be a phrase such as 'A full medical examination will be arranged'.

7 AVAILABILITY TO TRAVEL
This may include clean driver's license, own vehicle and willingness to travel or move to another city or country. The employer is looking for someone who is willing to be flexible.

8 PERSONALITY
The job profile may call for someone who is 'adaptable' or who can 'work well under pressure', or similar characteristics.

DESIRABLES

The desirable items are likely to be in the same type of areas as the essentials, but these are more open to negotiation. For example, a desirable skill might be familiarity with a particular software package.

It is not essential that you have used this, as your knowledge of other packages will demonstrate an ability to learn, but it will save time if are already familiar with it.

If you can demonstrate that you meet one or more of the desirables as well as the essentials, you have a better chance of success.

Looking at the qualities and experience that are essential and desirable also offers you the opportunity, prior to the interview, to review your pitch and tailor it both to deal with the gaps that may exist against the essentials and to try to fill the desirable elements as closely as possible.

who are you and what are you selling?

Reducing differentials

There are a number of ways to reduce the differences between your skills and experience and the job description. You can assume that you have met enough of the essentials to get to the first interview, but you need to check how you might get beyond that point.

Look at your CV and try to identify possible areas in which you may not have made the most of the experience you have had.

CONSIDER ALL PROJECTS

You may not have listed all the projects you were involved with in the course of one particular position – a CV is not necessarily the best place to do this. However, one or more of these projects may make your experience clear and make you a good fit for the position that is being offered.

INCLUDE TRAINING

Don't forget to include periods of on-the-job training. These not only demonstrate your willingness and capacity to learn but also show that previous employers felt that you were worth their investment in terms of time and money – these are good skills to have in your portfolio.

USE EXPERIENCE OUTSIDE WORK

Highlight the best of your entire experience in and out of the workplace. Something from a leisure pursuit – organizing a local charity's finances, for example, or other community activities – may also demonstrate your suitability for the position.

Do not invent experiences that you have not had. Just make the most of the time you have spent in other jobs. You can emphasize 'like' and 'near' experience, when you do not possess the exact experience to do the advertised job.

who are you and what are you selling?

Making negatives positives

Concentrate on what was achieved in each of your previous positions. In this way, you can start to identify and work on the areas in which you may not meet the requirements set out in the job profile.

BUILD ON ACHIEVEMENTS

Build on the positive achievements in each of your previous positions. A future employer is not necessarily interested in getting someone who totally matches the profile they have written: They want someone who will exceed the basic requirements and will be able to grow with the company and improve the profitability of the organization.

THINK ABOUT OUTCOMES

Concentrate on the outcomes of what you have done and listed on your CV, not necessarily what you did, and certainly not why you did it, but how you did it, and more importantly what was the result or outcome. These are your unique accomplishments and it is reasonable for a prospective employer to infer that you will achieve similar accomplishments if given the position that is open. You need to analyze these outcomes to match them as closely as possible to the various elements of the job profile.

Take some of the areas you have identified as your core skills and key achievements and analyze how the results can be interpreted to meet the needs identified in the profile. For example:

1 TEAM BUILDER
Emphasize the leadership you exerted to show how you can make a difference.

2 CONCEPTUALIZER
Report on your ideas that may have influenced future production (even if your idea was not the final product).

3 MENTOR
Think of roles in the business and personal spheres where you have been 'shadowed' or fulfilled a 'grandfather' role.

who are you and what are you selling?

Checklist: how do you match the job profile?

Look at everything you have done, and areas where you can negotiate around difficulties, and check off why you can fill the vacancy.

1 JOB PROFILE

Examples from your CV

☐

2 QUALIFICATIONS

Evidence of your skills base

☐

3 EXPERIENCE

Your familiarity and experience in your field

☐

4 APTITUDES

Your ability to liaise with others ☐

Your ability to use specific software ☐

5 PERSONAL SKILLS

Well organized ☐

Able to work under pressure ☐

CHECKLIST

Is this the right position/time/organization for me?

At this point, you have the time to think about the position more deeply.

YOU HAVE CLEARLY ESTABLISHED:

1 The company and its position in the marketplace.

2 The position within the company's structure.

3 What happened to the last person in the position.

4 Whether travel and nights away from home are routine/possible/unlikely.

5 Whether promotion is possible or likely.

6 The company ethos.

You also need to think about what you want from any job:

- Do you like teamwork?
- Do you dislike client contact?
- Do you like attracting work, or not?

Is financial reward all important, or would you rather be paid less to do something you really enjoy?

THEN YOU NEED TO THINK ABOUT WHAT YOU WANT:

1 Do you want to progress in this company?

2 Do you have other commitments that may mean you cannot give the position 100 percent?

3 Are you at a stage in your career when you don't want to move from project to project?

When you consider all of these points, you are checking that there is still a good match between you as the individual applying for the job and the position itself, not on the basis of your technical skills or experience level, but from your own personal viewpoint.

Knowing yourself: personality types

If you decide to go forward to the interview, you will need to analyze yourself as an individual.

■ What makes you tick?

■ What are you happiest doing?

■ Where do you work best?

■ What type of organizational creature are you?

You need to understand your own personality type in order to manage the interview process effectively and then fit into the position being offered.

Behavioral psychologists have identified four main character types, which make up the general population (and therefore the workforce). These groups are discussed more fully in Chapter 4 (see pp. 156–159).

1 LEADERS
CAPTAINS
CHAIRS:
If you always want to be first and lead the conversation or the team, then you are in this group.

2 TEAM WORKERS
GROUP WORKERS
SHARERS:
If you prefer to work with others in a team and like to share information, this is the set for you.

3 IDEAS PEOPLE:
If you always see the alternative way to do something or an option that no one else sees, then you belong to this group.

4 CHECKERS COMPLETER/FINISHERS:
If you pay attention to detail and the completion of a job is vital to you, then you belong in this group.

Thinking about the tasks you enjoy and the areas in which you have been most successful can help you to identify which of these groups you belong to and, therefore, the kinds of jobs you are most likely to get. If you are not an ideas person, you are unlikely to be successful in an interview for a job that involves coming up with new concepts and, even if you were to be successful, the chances are that you would not be satisfied doing the job.

who are you and what are you selling?

Your career values

Your relationship with work is likely to change as your career progresses, but everyone has a set of career values that underpin their working life.

Your background, upbringing and general philosophy of life have given you a value system, which you probably share with your close friends. Your values are what motivate you in your life and also in your career. You might value money, status or a certain lifestyle, for example. Perhaps money is not an issue but time to be with friends or travel is. Your values are the things you believe in and that are important to you.

A career that fits in with your value system is likely to motivate you to succeed; one that goes against your value system may be stressful or frustrating and will not be fulfilling.

UNDERSTANDING YOUR VALUES
Think about some of these statements and your responses to them to gain a greater understanding of your career values at this point.

1 What I like most about myself is...

2 My greatest personal achievement so far is...

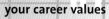

3 My greatest professional achievement so far is...

4 This year, I would like to...

5 By the end of my career, I would like to...

6 If I won the lottery, the first thing I would do is...

7 The worst thing that could happen to me is...

VALUES AND CAREER PLANNING
Think about the following areas
of your life and their relative
importance to you. Rate them
on a scale of 1 to 5; 5 for those
that are truly important to you,
scaling down to 1 for those that
do not really interest you:

SOCIAL FACTORS
■ Honesty, equality
■ Peace, harmony
■ Justice
■ Security

INTELLECTUAL FACTORS
■ Pursuit of knowledge
■ Personal growth
■ Ability to understand

PERSONAL FACTORS
■ Family life
■ Travel
■ Friendship
■ Material wealth
  and comfort
■ Self respect

CAREER
■ Leadership, power
■ Recognition: by peers,
  by wider community
■ Risk
■ Stability

UNDERSTANDING YOUR VALUES

1 Which are the values you marked with a 5?

2 Which rated a 1?

3 Are there jobs you couldn't do because of your values?

4 The key is to get a job that matches most of your 5s, and does not centre around your 1s.

who are you and what are you selling?

Your career commercial

Like any other commercial, a career commercial is selling a product – your career commercial is selling you.

When you sell yourself, you are selling a product that you already know. You should start to put together your career commercial from your known abilities. Your commercial should encompass who you are and the benefits your core abilities and attributes will bring to the organization, both now and in the future.

EIGHT AREAS TO COVER IN YOUR CAREER COMMERCIAL:

1 WHO I AM
How you refer to yourself

2 MY BACKGROUND
Your professional history

3 I HAVE WORKED WITH
Your clients and previous employers

4 MY ACCOMPLISHMENTS
The highlights of your career to date

5 MY MAJOR STRENGTHS
Your memorable qualities

6 MY PERSONAL QUALITIES
What shapes you

7 EDUCATION AND TRAINING
What has really made you
different from others with
your general background

8 MY FUTURE
Where you want to
position yourself in your
chosen field

CREATING YOUR CAREER COMMERCIAL:

1 Make it brief: this is not a commentary on your CV.

2 Keep it conversational.

3 Be familiar and comfortable with it.

Your career commercial is your ideal chance to pinpoint who you are, what
you do and what your value will be to the organization.

who are you and what are you selling?

Checklist: developing your USP

Your Unique Selling Proposition (USP) is what is going to sell you to a
company. It's what makes you unique and different from every other
candidate. When you have looked at your skills and experience, use this
checklist to put your USP together.

1   Compatibility with the company – from your research

2   THE PROBLEMS I CAN SOLVE FOR THE ORGANIZATION

Financial

Technical

Public image

3   THE THINGS I DO REALLY WELL

Lead

Ideas

4 MY MAJOR CAREER ACHIEVEMENTS TO DATE

Implemented

Undertaken

5 THE UNUSUAL THINGS I HAVE DONE AND CAN DO

Work-related accomplishments

Special skills

All of these add up to a compelling set of qualifications that you can offer a potential employer when nobody else can.

Dealing with problem areas

You will by now be identifying the areas of your CV that do not meet the job profile or parts of the job description you have identified as important.

EXAMPLES:

PROBLEMS:	POSSIBLE SOLUTIONS:
Rapid position changes	Gained varied experience in a short timeframe
Bad press	Learned from the problems of organization and developed own skills
Gaps in employment	Waited for right opportunity and took time out to improve skills by studying (with specifics on qualifications)

PROBLEMS:	POSSIBLE SOLUTIONS:
Periods out of the workforce	Took time to look after children or care for elderly relative, used free time to develop additional skills (detailing what they were)
Sudden changes of career	Necessary to change location due to promotion of partner so responsible for relocating family and had to look for alternative position (make any changes sound considered and planned; add specifics)

who are you and what are you selling?

Preparing your answers

There are several basic questions that an interviewer is likely to ask and that you can prepare for before the interview.

1 What is your current job?

2 Tell us about yourself?

3 Why do you want this job?

4 What is the most important thing for you in a job?

5 What is your greatest strength?

6 What is your greatest weakness?

These are the questions that interviewers tend to fall back on. You need to work out convincing answers that don't sound too rehearsed.

Draw on the information in your CV and the pitch that demonstrates your USP for material to answer these questions.

My current job is...
(then go on to demonstrate the items you want to emphasize):

■ Has given me more leadership experience

example: able to improve team spirit

outcome: reduced staff turnover

■ Has offered me different challenges

example: worked in different locations in company

outcome: greater knowledge of industry

I am the sort of person who...
(look to bring out your USP):

■ Likes new challenges

example: able to implement new ideas

outcome: reduced rejections on the grounds of quality

■ Needs to be part of a team

example: placed into a team that was failing and turned it around

outcome: worked to make team most productive in division

I want this job because...
(here you can bring in
information from your research):

■ I am interested in your
   company

– include an example: e.g.
I want to be involved in
developments I have read about

– don't forget the outcome: e.g.
I will be able to make the same
improvements to your systems as
I made at my last company

■ I am aware of how you
   approach a subject

– include an example: e.g.
your last project

– don't forget the outcome: e.g.
improvements that you made

The most important thing for
me in a job is... (bring in some
detail from your CV):

■ The chance to work on projects
   that benefit different groups
   in society

– include an example: e.g.
a project that I undertook

– don't forget the outcome: e.g.
improved the housing conditions
of people in the local district

My greatest strength:

■ My enthusiasm

– include an example of when this made a difference: e.g. implemented a new procedure ahead of schedule by demonstrating to the whole team how it would be of benefit to all of us

– don't forget the outcome: e.g. the result was a saving of several thousand dollars a quarter for the group and substantial time savings on routine tasks for all workers

My greatest weakness:

■ My time management skills need improving...

– include an example of when this lack of skills was apparent: e.g. ran out of time on a major project because I didn't plan my time carefully

– don't forget the outcome: e.g. mention action you are taking to improve the situation

Focusing on achievements

Draw out the major issues to accentuate the positive achievements
from your career history.

SYSTEMATICALLY EVALUATE:

1 What the job or assignment was.

2 What actions you took to combat the problems you identified
or were asked to solve.

3 What the outcome was: a saving or reduction in cost or
improvement in staff morale (demonstrate by a reduction
in turnover).

Although you should stick to the truth, there are many ways of selling your
success to get your message across such as how you saved the company
money (see opposite page).

OUTCOME EXAMPLES:

YOU HAD A POSITION WITH A LIMITED BUDGET

By your actions, you reduced a previous overspend. Don't dwell on the absolute value, but use a percentage – saving 25 percent sounds far better than saving 250 pounds or dollars on a budget of 1000 pounds or dollars.

YOU IMPLEMENTED A STAFF REDUCTION

Detail how you managed to cut staff costs, perhaps by redeployment in another department or at another site.

Be prepared to elaborate on answers, but try to leave the interviewer wanting more – make your answers concise and leave space for follow-up.

Positive selling

As you work on your answers to likely questions, use positive action words to say what you have done. Some of these words will not fit your industry, but think along these lines.

Accelerated	Constructed	Facilitated
Adapted	Coordinated	Focused
Analyzed	Decreased	Formulated
Attracted	Designed	Fostered
Balanced	Developed	Galvanized
Befriended	Directed	Grew
Benefitted	Enhanced	Implemented
Budgeted	Established	Improved
Completed	Exceeded	Initiated
Conceived	Executed	Managed

Mentored	Promoted	Tabled
Motivated	Promulgated	Targeted
Negotiated	Recruited	Terminated
Nurtured	Redesigned	Transferred
Officiated	Researched	Undertook
Opened	Restructured	Unified
Optimized	Solved	
Organized	Sourced	
Planned	Stratified	
Profited	Succeeded	

who are you and what are you selling?

As the interview approaches

Whatever its format, as the interview approaches, you need to be fully prepared. You should have an understanding of the following points:

AN UNDERSTANDING OF THE ORGANIZATION

- The type of organization
- Where it sits in the marketplace
- How it is positioned in the industry
- What the development potential is

AN UNDERSTANDING OF WHAT THE ORGANIZATION WANTS

- The level of the position in the structure
- The next position you might be expected to move to after the one you are applying for
- What happened to the last holder of the position

AN UNDERSTANDING OF YOURSELF

- The elements of your CV that you want to emphasize
- Ways of disguising or minimizing problem areas
- Your USP
- What you are able to bring to the position

With this information, you also have to consider the style of the organization and what is termed the 'best fit' personality – the person who not only fits with the position's essentials and desirables on the job profile but who will also fit with the company (from the research you carried out).

EXPERIENCE OUTSIDE WORK

It can help to present you as a 'rounded' individual if you talk about attributes and interests that are not solely work-related. However, this can be counterproductive.

Anything that might have an impact on your ability to get the job done (such as having to leave on time each evening or regularly traveling on weekends) is likely to sound warning bells to a potential employer.

Despite legislation, discrimination goes on all the time at all levels of the labour market. So don't volunteer personal information about marital status, children, religion, even hobbies, unless you know from your research or from a company visit that it is going to help your application.

Checklist: getting the right position

1 Research the marketplace, the company and the position.

2 Know your own strengths and get them across during the interview.

3 Be on time, appropriately dressed and uncluttered.

4 Treat the interview as a two-way exchange of information.

5 Offer evidence-based answers that indicate that you can do the job.

6 Convey enthusiasm for the organization and the position.

7 Use the interview to decide whether you actually want the job.

8 Keep your answers short and to the point.

9 Don't negotiate a salary or benefits package in the interview.

10 Thank every person involved in the interview process, in writing.

CHECKLIST

3

interview essentials

Interview scenarios

The word 'interview' covers anything from an informal chat to a two- or three-day series of tests and exercises, and several scenarios in between.

The higher up the corporate ladder you climb, and the more important it becomes for employers to find the right person for their openings, the more likely you are to have to negotiate your way through several phases of the interview process. Here are some possible interview scenarios and ways of getting through them to the next stage of the process.

At every stage, you should show a willingness to participate fully in the process, taking on any assignments and tasks with enthusiasm and professionalism.

INFORMAL CONVERSATION

A recruitment advertisement might invite interested candidates to call and talk through a possible opening, or to go in to an office for a look around and discuss openings informally. Once you have seen the operational setup and had this conversation, you might decide to put in a formal application or you might be put off the company.

FORMAL INTERVIEW

You send in your CV or fill out an application form and you are invited for an interview. This may be a 'one-off', after which you might be offered the job, but it is more likely to be the first big hurdle in securing the position. This is the occasion to sell yourself and ask questions to determine if this is really where you want to be. Generally, a formal interview might be with one interviewer, possibly the line manager for the position, a recruiter or someone from HR.

PRESENTATION

On the strength of your performance at interview, you might be asked to make a presentation to more of the senior executives, for example, or head a lecture, or lead a training session in a particular piece of hardware or software. The interview probably showed you were the right type of person for the position, but this more focused exercise is designed to show you have the personal skills as well as the background knowledge and presentation skills to handle the challenges of the position.

SECOND INTERVIEW

You may not have to make a presentation, but few jobs these days are decided on a one-shot interview. The most likely scenario is that you have a formal interview and then get invited back to talk more. This is your chance to make sure you are offered the position. You can ask more searching questions about the organization and its goals, your likely contribution to the organization's future success, and financial and other packages. Use this slightly more relaxed atmosphere to find out all you can about the organization and its employees.

MEET POTENTIAL COLLEAGUES

The company is seriously interested by now, and you are invited to meet the team. This is not senior management, these are the people you might be working with on a daily basis. Are they open and friendly? Do you sense any hostility? Does someone not join a group lunch? Who is the joker? Who is uptight? This is the ideal opportunity to decide if the position is right for you: can you see yourself heading up or fitting into this team?

TEAM-BUILDING EXERCISE

The company might be employing a whole new team. It's possible that they have 20 candidates whom they are interested in and they want to get a dynamic, effective team of five people to work together. Be aware that you are under constant scrutiny in this type of exercise, and use all your skills in watching the group dynamics (see pp. 156–159).

Whatever the scenario(s), your task is to get to the next hurdle successfully, or – remembering that interviews are a two-way process – to decide that this is not the right position for you at this time.

NOTE

This chapter deals with a formal one-on-one interview scenario. More detailed information on panel interviews, presentations and assessment centre interviews and social aspects of interviews are covered in Chapter 4.

Presenting yourself

Behavioural studies have shown that interviewers make up their minds about candidates quickly. This may not be a good thing, but it is a fact that the first impression you make when entering the interview room is crucial.

WARDROBE
Generally, the research you have done on the company should give you some idea of an appropriate wardrobe for your interview. A pre-interview visit to the offices or facility will also give you valuable information about any dress code.

A suit and tie for men and suit and smart shirt for women are still a fairly safe bet, but if you have clearly established that the organization has an informal dress code, be wary of arriving for the interview looking too formal and out of place.

In many knowledge-based or creative organizations, a degree of informality is taken as a sign of an individual's ability to think 'outside the box', and in marketing or media-orientated organizations, designer or 'smart–casual' clothing is often regarded as the norm.

COMFORT

Whatever you wear, you will need to feel comfortable, so make sure everything fits correctly: avoid tight new shoes or other items that will lead you to concentrate on your own discomfort rather than allowing you to focus on your performance.

BACK TO BASICS

A small outlay for a new shirt might be a worthwhile investment to give the right finishing effect to a suit. Similarly, a new tie or scarf might make you stand out from the rest of the pack wearing dark suits.

It is a good idea to prepare your clothes several days before the interview – it may have slipped your mind that something needs to be dry-cleaned or needs a button replacing, for example.

SOME BASIC POINTS TO REMEMBER:

1 Your outfit should be clean, smart and not creased.

2 Clothing that is too tight looks unprofessional.

3 Clothing that is too large will make you appear lost and vague, even if you are not.

4 Be sure your shoes are in good repair and properly polished. Heels should not be worn down.

PERSONAL GROOMING

It goes without saying that your general appearance should be neat and clean, so hair, nails and teeth need attention prior to the interview. Unless your research shows the organization to be highly informal, very bright nail polish, off-the-wall hair colour and ostentatious body piercings and tattoos are not a good idea. Keeping jewellery neutral can also pay dividends. An interviewer who is fascinated by your dangling earrings is not going to be listening to what you have to say on a serious subject.

BAGS AND LUGGAGE

Carrying items to the interview should be carefully considered. You want to appear as uncluttered as possible. If you need a handbag or case to hold materials for a presentation, make sure it is small and can be easily placed aside to free your hands for introductions. If you have to take a larger case for an overnight stay, try to leave it in the reception area or in an outer office before entering the interview room. This also applies to coats, jackets and umbrellas.

Arrive in good time

Nothing gives a bad impression to potential employers than a late arrival for an interview. Even if you arrive just in time, you may appear flustered and breathless, so leave yourself plenty of time.

For your own peace of mind and to make a better impression, be early and use the time to prepare yourself so that you are calm and relaxed as you enter the room for the interview. You can also use the time to make sure your grooming is immaculate and to safely store any outerwear and luggage that you won't need in the interview.

If you are traveling by public transport, give yourself plenty of time for missed connections or delays. If you are driving your own car, remember to allow enough time to find somewhere to park and to walk from there to the interview location.

PREPARE IN ADVANCE:

1 Check the exact location of the place at which you have been instructed to attend. You don't want to rush from the reception to the fifth floor when the lift is out of service.

2 If the interview is in a city with which you are unfamiliar, get a map – don't rely on a taxi driver knowing the business' address, or the way.

3 When you arrive, make sure the appropriate person knows you are there.

4 Switch off your mobile phone.

The first few seconds

Many employers make decisions in the first minute of the interview. The impression you make as you enter the room and introduce yourself can be vital to your success.

You are probably going to be nervous but you can use the adrenaline to your advantage to give your best possible performance. If you have practiced what you are going to say, use the energy rush to a positive advantage. There is no point in being the best candidate if you don't get your message across. It is also worth remembering that any other candidates are likely to be nervous, too. It could well come down to who controls their nerves best.

1 Concentrate on the introduction so that you know the name and position of the person interviewing you.

2 Establish eye contact.

3 A smile is your best asset to making a good impression.

4 Try to relax; keep breathing deeply to help settle any nerves.

5 If the room is set up for an across-the-desk meeting, you may have to accept this, but if there is a choice of seats, try to sit so that you are about 45 degrees to the interviewer. This allows you to initiate a good dialogue.

Listening to the agenda

You may have been sent an 'agenda' for the interview, or it may be outlined before the interview itself starts (or you might have been sent an agenda that will be recapped at the beginning of the interview). Whichever is the case, concentrate on what is being said and be prepared to respond appropriately.

If you want to take notes, ask if this is acceptable to the interviewer. This is especially useful if you need to remember directions to other rooms or locations for further parts of the assessment process. Be positive about wanting to get the information right – it's better to ask for details again than to miss something important.

The downside of note taking is that it can make the conversation stilted, so consider this before you decide. If you do not answer a question or make a point, or even worse if you mishear or misunderstand a question, because you are writing, it can be counterproductive. It might be more appropriate to ask for clarification of one or two points at the end of the interview, than to take your focus away from what the interviewer is saying, and how you are responding.

Usually you will have some idea of how the interview will be structured, but you may not, so be prepared with information of your own and with the points you want to get across. If the interviewer does not outline a time for your questions, for example, ask when they would be appropriate.

The assessment process starts as soon as you enter the room so be ready to be in active listening mode when you enter. Remember that the interview is a two-way process – you want to gain information on the organization just as much as they want information from you. Ideally, you will be asking questions throughout, gradually building up a mental picture of what it would be like to work for this company in these offices.

Active and reflective listening

The main process of the interview is for questions to be asked and your responses considered. Ideally, there is no hidden agenda. The interviewer wants to give you the opportunity to demonstrate your skills and experience.

To give yourself the best chance you need to listen effectively:

1 Be prepared to listen.

2 Be interested and attentive.

3 Interpret the question if you need to.

4 Be sure that you understand the question.

HEAR THE QUESTION OUT

Don't jump in to answer a question before you have heard it out. Wait until the interviewer has finished.

Listen to every word, understand what is being asked, and wait for the natural space for your response.

Be prepared to ask for clarification of a question – it may give you the time you need to order your thoughts and to develop your answer.

ACKNOWLEDGE THAT YOU ARE REALLY LISTENING

While the question is being asked or information is being given, show that you are following and understanding.

This type of reflective listening is signaled with verbal responses such as 'I see', 'Right' or 'Yes'.

PARAPHRASE THE QUESTION TO ANSWER IT

On occasions you should preface your answer by paraphrasing the question to ensure that you have correctly interpreted what the interviewer is asking.

Phrases such as ' You are asking...' or ' Am I right in thinking...' show that you have listened and are carefully thinking about the question you have been asked.

Objection vs rejection

An interviewer might ask a tough question: Why have you changed jobs so frequently? What makes you think your experience to date is relevant for this position? The point to remember is that, in asking the question, there is a desire to hear what you have to say. The interviewer is not rejecting your application but is raising an objection to it. If you can handle objections effectively, you can still get the job.

HANDLING OBJECTIONS

1

SELL WHAT YOU WILL BRING
Your career commercial and accomplishment statement should enable you to get all the benefits you will bring across. The more you bring, the fewer objections the interviewer will raise.

2

LISTEN TO THE CONCERN
Hear the objection out. Never assume that you know what the question is going to be. When you have heard the objection out, frame your answer, along the lines of 'I'm pleased to have the opportunity to clarify that...' or 'I understand that might be a concern...'. Then give your answer.

3 TURN AN OBJECTION INTO A QUESTION
An interviewer might raise an objection along the lines of 'You don't seem to have much experience of...'. Note the underlying question and answer it.

4 BE CLEAR ABOUT WHAT THE OBJECTION IS
Be sure you understand the objection. Is it that you really are overqualified for a position, or is there a fear that you will want too much money, for example.

5 CONFIRM YOUR ANSWER
Be sure that you have indeed refuted the objection. 'Does that answer your concerns in this area?' If it doesn't, you have invited the interviewer to say so and given yourself another opportunity to allay any misgivings.

interview essentials

Answering questions

An interviewer is likely to ask questions to find out about your personality, skills and experience. Answering the question is key to your success.

GIVE CLEAR CONCISE ANSWERS:

1 Always have your selling points in mind and be sure to give answers that are consistent with your CV or application form.

2 Always answer the question truthfully, but be sure you know the reason behind the question.

AS A GENERAL RULE, DON'T ANSWER ANY QUESTION THAT YOU DON'T
FULLY UNDERSTAND:

1   Ask for clarification, and don't give any information

until you know what is being asked for.

2   If you think a question is rather vague and you could

answer it in several ways, ask for clarification: 'You

are referring in particular to...' and 'You are asking about

my time with...' are good 'reflectors' to unclear questions.

WHEN ANSWERING QUESTIONS:

1 Maintain eye contact, but do not stare.

2 Don't fidget: it distracts from your message. If you are nervous, rest your hands on the desk in front of you.

3 Avoid extravagant gestures, but be prepared to use your hands to emphasize important points. Think of politicians and the way they use body language and hand movements to reinforce their messages.

4 If you tend to be nervous, ask someone you trust to rehearse your answers with you so that you are confident in their message and content before the event.

5 Avoid exaggeration, even though it may be tempting. Give a concise answer and wait for a secondary question before giving further examples.

Critical to your success at the interview is your ability to back up your answers with specific examples. These will come from the work you have done on your unique selling proposition (see pp. 66–67) and on the themes that run through your career path.

Avoid rambling

Sometimes in the interview situation, nerves will out, with the result that your mouth runs away with you. The work anecdote that seems amusing when chatting socially with friends can demonstrate a potential lack of seriousness and may well backfire on you during an interview. Don't be afraid of a pause in the conversation: It is not your responsibility to fill it.

The trick is to use any nervous energy for your own ends. Be aware that stress (and no matter how chatty the process seems, an interview is stressful) will:

1 Increase your heart rate

2 Quicken your breathing

3 Increase the likelihood that you will sweat, particularly in your palms

The best way to deal with a tendency to ramble is to be prepared for it. Do not be so stiff with responses that you sound like a robot giving the 'right' answers on cue, but have in your mind a set of responses that will paint you in the best possible light (see pp. 70–75). It can be difficult to remember that the interview is a social event: it is better that there is a pause in the conversation than that you start to lose your nerve through rambling.

Most of your responses will be based around your USP and career commercial. So you should have a concise understanding of five or six key strengths or skills that the interviewer is going to want to hear about, with relevant experience to back these up, and prepare short examples of the outcome of and benefits from your actions in any previous role.

If you have done your research carefully, you should not find yourself faced with a question that you simply cannot answer. If you find a question difficult to answer, it is always worth repeating it back to the interviewer to give yourself a little more time to put together a coherent response.

Visual and nonverbal clues

We all give visual and non-verbal clues to what we are thinking in our everyday life. In a one-on-one interview, you need to be aware of what the interviewer is thinking.

1 A smile is normally a good sign.

2 A nod is a sign of recognition.

3 Comments or signs of active listening such as 'Go on' or 'I see' are useful indicators to you that your message is being received.

4 Don't panic if the interviewer is not responding, but try to add some emphasis to the points you make to ensure that you remain memorable.

5 If the interviewer leans forward, it may well be a sign of interest, but be sure you are speaking clearly and loudly enough – it may equally be a sign of irritation.

6 Unfocused eyes, a look at a wristwatch or a glance toward the door are signs that you are losing the interviewer. Finish your point quickly and work hard with your next response to get the interviewer back with you.

7 Be aware if something you say causes the interviewer to look again at your application or CV. Be prepared for a follow-up question to clarify an apparent contradiction between what you have just said and what is in your written information.

interview essentials
Body language

The way you enter the room, the way you stand, how you shake someone's hand and the way you sit during the interview all combine to say a lot about you. It is important that you understand this, without being paralyzed by it.

Don't try to be someone you are not. If your natural self is very outgoing, don't try to hide this away but be wary of its potentially overpowering effect. If you are reserved, don't try to be an extrovert, but use this to show that you are thoughtful and intelligent and are considering your answers.

Your research should have given you a strong feeling about the type of person the company wants for this position and the sort of people the company normally employs. So be aware of this and tailor your persona to be a good fit.

Employers are looking for energy from new employees so no matter how laid back you are normally, make an effort to be really upbeat and positive to leave a good impression.

SOME BASICS OF POSITIVE BODY LANGUAGE:

1 Remain relaxed. When standing, keep your weight balanced.

2 Don't grab at the interviewer's hand – a firm handshake is best.

3 Sit in a relaxed position, but do not slump into the chair.

4 Hand gestures convey animation or enthusiasm.

5 Keep your breathing deep and rhythmic. This will also help to keep nerves at bay and to make your speech firm and audible.

6 Try to match the body language of the interviewer. Do not mimic, but complement, so if the interviewer leans forward to ask a question, lean forward as you answer.

7 Leaning forward tends to indicate that someone is listening attentively.

Appropriate use of humour

A humorous story told in a bar after work may often be a good ice-breaker but the same story at interview can be completely inappropriate.

The best advice is to use humour sparingly, if at all, at interview. Even if you think it will not backfire, only use it when you are quite sure of the attitude of the interviewer, perhaps towards the end of the interview rather than at the beginning, when there is a certain level of the unknown between the two of you.

USE HUMOUR:

1 When you are trying to convey your own assurance in answering a question.

2 When relating an incident in answer to a question about your abilities.

BE WARY OF USING HUMOUR:

1 When it reflects badly on your ability or judgment (however, it can be used with care to convey your ability to understand and learn from mistakes or errors of judgment). Always try to ensure that the outcome from the story, although comic, is positive.

This is an area where a 'dry run' with someone who knows you can be invaluable. A person who knows the story already can give valuable feedback on how it might come across during an interview with someone who does not know you.

Taking charge of the interview

You know the points you want to get across at the interview and the best way to do so. If the interviewer is not allowing you to get your message across, you need to take charge.

RAMBLING QUESTIONS

Rambling answers (see pp. 106–107), like rambling questions will break up the flow of the interview and will not serve the purpose of the interview – to question a candidate, hear answers, and reach a decision on hiring. If the interviewer becomes lost in the question, the best way to respond is to try to reflect the question back to figure out the interviewer's intention. Phrases such as 'If I understand that correctly...' or 'Are you specifically referring to my time at XYZ...' may be what you need in this situation to move the interview along.

MULTIPLE QUESTIONS

An interviewer may be unaware of doing this, but in trying to cover everything, there is a tendency to run two or more questions together. The intention might be 'helpful', but in fact it is not. Try to reflect back and make it clear that there are two different questions and that you intend to answer both of them. Turn the situation to your advantage by asking for the second part of the question to be repeated to give you more time to consider your response.

THE WEIRD OR OFF-THE-WALL QUESTION

This may come from an interviewer who likes the sound of his or her own voice and is not giving you much chance to participate. Be careful not to be drawn into this process because it could mean that you don't get the points you need to discuss out in the open. At the point when you are able to get a word in, acknowledge what has been said and relate the discussion to your own experiences and the points you wanted to emphasize. 'I'd like to answer that by discussing my employment at...' or 'Perhaps I could answer that by telling you about...' are good openings.

THE HYPOTHETICAL SITUATION

Questions that pose hypothetical situations are often used to assess your poise, your ability to think 'on your feet', and how your mind works. You could ask for clarification of the question to give yourself time to think.

Types of interview questions

Before looking at how to answer the questions you might be asked, it is useful to know about the different types of questions.

OPEN QUESTIONS

Open questions normally require more than a 'Yes' or 'No' answer. They are usually prefaced by:

- Who?
- What?
- Where?
- When?
- How?

These questions will allow you to develop your case.

CLOSED QUESTIONS

Closed questions normally do not encourage further discussion. These invite a one-word answer:

- Which of these?
- How many?
- How often?

ANSWERING THE QUESTIONS

- Use action-based answers. Try to use the information you have amassed to drive your answers.

- Make sure that the actions you have taken in previous situations are the hooks on which you hang your answers.

- Try to leave the questioner wanting more – do not be overly long in your response.

WHAT NOT TO SAY

■ Don't run down your current boss or organization, or any previous ones. Most industries are small, and odds are that an interviewer knows or at least knows of your current employer and may have worked with or for them in the past.

■ Be circumspect about your current situation. If you are disloyal to your current organization, how is the prospective employer to know that you won't act in the same way about them?

■ Don't inflate your experience or position. It is so easy to check by phone or email, and any trained interviewer will find the truth fast.

■ Don't make up or inflate your qualifications. Again, it is too easy and fast to check.

■ It is not advisable to make up interests that you don't have. The first question by someone who really does pursue a hobby you invent will expose your bluff.

Checklist: answering questions

WHEN TALKING ABOUT YOURSELF, YOU CAN REFER TO THE USP THAT YOU
HAVE DEVELOPED:

1 My career follows a number of paths.

2 Running through all my previous posts.

3 I prefer to work with other people and you
can see from my last two jobs I have
managed to do that.

4 I am a thorough worker and always want to get the details right.

5 I like to be challenged to come up with new ideas and approaches.

6 Team-building is what I do best.

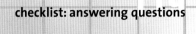

CHECKLIST

Then after making the responses on pp. 118–119, remember to give examples from your CV. Below are some examples:

1 When I was in charge of the team given

the task of...

2 My last manager asked me to devise a new

system for filing...

3 I have always liked working with different teams

so when I was asked to go to another site and

build up the teams there...

Always give examples of the outcome of your actions with the benefits that the organization gained. Benefits are best expressed in terms of revenue gained, time or money saved, or productivity or efficiency increased.

1

Increased turnover in my section by 25 percent.

Reduced staff turnover by 20 percent.

2

Increased market share by 10 percent.

3

Reduced waiting time for patients below targets.

4

Improved responses to clients by 100 percent.

CHECKLIST

Handling inappropriate questions

In spite of tough legislation designed to stamp out discrimination on a number of grounds, some interviewers still ask questions that they should not.

There are areas of your private life that, by law, prospective employers should not ask about. These are:

■ Marital status

■ Religion

■ Sexual orientation

■ Childcare arrangements

■ Disabilities

■ Race or ethnicity

In addition, there are areas that are hardly appropriate for discussion at the interview and although interviewers may ask you questions, it might be more appropriate to be circumspect in answering them:

■ Age

■ Gender issues

■ Health issues

DEFLECTING INAPPROPRIATE QUESTIONS

Despite training, legislation, and best efforts, some interviewers still ask politically incorrect questions. If this happens:

■ You need to stay calm.

■ You should ask if the question is being put to all candidates. This may awaken recognition of how inappropriate the question is.

■ An answer that states the facts and makes it clear that there is no issue to be answered should combat such questions.

Although you should not be asked inappropriate questions, you may need to be prepared to deflect them. You might ask for clarification of the question to give the interviewer the chance to retract it.

Questions to ask at a first interview

The interview is a two-way process, and you need to ask as well as answer questions. These are the areas that your questions should cover over the course of the interview.

ABOUT THE POSITION:

- Is the position newly established?

- How many other managers are there on the same level?

- Does the person who takes the position report directly to a board-level executive?

- Is there a system for setting objectives for the position?

ABOUT THE ORGANIZATION:

- Do you have an internal training system?

- Is there a system for appraisal?

- Does the company support employees to take college or lifelong learning courses?

ABOUT THE SUPPORT THE POSITION IS GIVEN:

- Is there a team in place?

- Will I be encouraged to recruit my own team?

- What level of technical support is in place for IT or financial systems?

- What administrative support is in place?

ABOUT THE FINANCIAL ACCOUNTABILITY OF THE POSITION:

- What level of autonomy will the person who is hired for this position have?

- To whom will the new employee report on financial matters?

- How often are reports made?

Questions not to ask at a first interview

Here are some areas to avoid at the initial interview. Wait until you are considering a firm offer.

SALARY

Avoid talking money at the first meeting. You will probably be aware of the sort of level the position has in the organization, and this will reflect the kind of salary that will be offered.

Don't start discussing salary until a job offer has been made. This will mean that there is already an investment in you and a few percentage points on the salary are less likely to be a major issue. Also by the time you get to discuss money, you will have convinced the organization's representatives that you will be bringing added value above what you will cost.

If salary is raised early in the process by the interviewer be wary. It is better to fend off the question by commenting that is too soon to say how much you have to offer the company.

BENEFITS

Salary and benefits are similar: you don't want to discuss benefits too early. Wait until an offer has been made.

You might open negotiations on benefits when you have a clear picture as to what the salary is. Also you will know how eager the employer is to get you and can start to build up the package.

HOLIDAY ALLOWANCES

Paid or unpaid holiday time varies enormously. Have some ideas on what you want or need, but, again, this is not a subject to raise at a first interview. Wait for an offer— you are more likely to get what you want.

BONUSES/COMMISSION

In some cases, the question of bonus may be covered in the original advertisement for the position. However, you should wait until a job offer is on the table and then discuss the whole remuneration package.

If you are an internal candidate

On the face of it, this seems the ideal situation. You probably know the interviewer and he or she knows you. You should also have knowledge of the organization and an understanding of its goals and aims.

THERE ARE, HOWEVER, PITFALLS THAT CAN TRIP YOU UP:

1 Your reputation precedes you.

2 Be wary of trading on misplaced loyalty.

3 The position might call for 'a breath of fresh air' or new ideas from an outsider, so don't fall into the trap of 'I know the company and its products'.

Check your understanding of the company's goals: these may have changed or be changing. This position may be for a catalyst to alter the future of the company. If this is the case and you're sounding wedded to the status quo, you are unlikely to be offered the position.

Try to approach the interview objectively, as if you were an outsider looking in.

Do the research on the company as if you did not know it – you will probably come up with some useful insights that you might otherwise have missed.

If you're up against an internal candidate

When you are an outsider invited for an interview, it is advisable to sell the fact that you are different and can bring fresh ideas into the company.

Some organizations recruit to see what kind of talent is available in the marketplace in comparison with the staff they already have. Often, however, an external candidate has an advantage. If an internal candidate were truly appointable, the organization would not be going through the expense, in both time and money, of recruitment.

Coming to an organization from outside also gives you the ability to bring new ideas and alternative strategies to the business. You have already shown some of these to get invited for the interview, and you will demonstrate more at the interview itself.

You are demonstrating your commitment to career advancement: you have applied for a position with a new organization. However, be aware that the business community is relatively parochial – even though you are the outside candidate an interviewer may well have knowledge of your current employer, your current work and professional and even personal information about you.

Always use the fact that you are the outsider to demonstrate bringing to the organization new ways of doing things or innovations from a different sector. Use the positive advantage of difference to generate a feeling that the organization needs your new ideas, and match this to the issues that you know – from your research – are important to them.

Wrapping up an interview

As the interview draws to a close, there are some points you need to be absolutely clear about so if they are not offered, be sure to ask.

1 THE NEXT STEP

If this is a first conversation about an opening

that is real and current, what is the next step in the

process before the company decides on a candidate

to fill the position?

2 TIMEFRAME

When will candidates hear whether the company is

still interested?

3 A POSITIVE LAST IMPRESSION

Reaffirm your positive feelings about the company and

the position, mention that everything you have heard at

the interview reinforces the research you had done, restate

why you want to work there and say that you look forward

to hearing about the next stage of the process.

4 SAY 'THANK YOU'

Finally, thank the interviewer, offer a firm handshake, and leave.

Checklist: after the interview

As soon as you get home, think about your performance. Fit this checklist to your own business area. Some of these may not apply to you.

TECHNICAL

1 I had all the skills needed. ☐

2 I handled the questions about X software OK, but it was probably clear to the interviewer that I hadn't used it much. ☐

3 The question about the X really threw me. ☐

ACADEMIC

1 The company clearly wanted someone with a qualification in... ☐

2 I haven't published enough papers. ☐

SKILLS

1 My people skills will be an asset. ☐

2 The fact that I demonstrated I could analyze financial data was good. ☐

EXPERIENCE

1 I think I did enough for their current needs. ☐

2 The fact that I've never worked for a company employing more than 20 people is going to count against me. ☐

3 They wanted someone with more retail experience. ☐

4 I haven't had enough management experience. ☐

THE INTERVIEW ITSELF

1 I answered all the questions well. ☐

2 I did start to ramble, but I pulled it back. ☐

3 The joke was a mistake. ☐

4 The finance guy didn't like me. ☐

5 I didn't get answers to some key questions. ☐

6 The fact that it was a long interview could be good or bad. Did I lose the point? Was the interviewer even interested? ☐

7 It's a good sign that we discussed notice periods. ☐

8 All the questions were focused and relevant. ☐

9 We got a good dialogue going. ☐

If you get an offer, you probably don't need self-appraisal, but if you are unsuccessful, it can be useful: you have some sort of framework when asking for feedback (see pp. 220–223), and you can avoid the obvious mistakes at your next interview.

CHECKLIST

Starting your follow-up

Evidence suggests that only 5 percent of jobseekers send a thank you letter after an interview, yet this is an excellent tool.

1 It reminds the interviewer of who you are.

2 It gives you an opportunity to make another pitch.

3 It reinforces your interest in the organization and the position.

4 It acknowledges that the interviewer took time out of a busy day to meet with you.

There are three basic approaches:

EMAIL
Some companies rely heavily on e-mail, and this may be the most appropriate approach. It is certainly fast, so you can write the same day, and it is useful if you know a decision is to made quickly. There are two possible objections. The first is that it is informal and may not be appropriate for some organizations. The second is that some individuals receive so many emails in a day that yours will not stand out.

HANDWRITTEN NOTE
If the interview was fairly informal and you felt that there was a real rapport, a handwritten note might be appropriate. It is personal and one-on-one, and if this is what you believe the position being offered calls for, take this approach.

BUSINESS LETTER
A typed letter is best if the organization is formal, or if you are really not sure what would be most appropriate.

If you send a letter by mail, aim to write it that same day so that no more than a day or two passes between the interview and the letter's arrival. If you are interviewed by more than one person, write to them all.

Your letter should thank the people involved for their time, express your interest in hearing about the position and briefly recap what you would bring to it.

4

in-depth interview scenarios

Finding out more about you

At the heart of most interview processes is a one-on-one interview, as described in chapter 3. However, it is increasingly common for potential employers to do the following:

1 Organize a series of one-on-one interviews, after which interviewers 'pool' opinions to select the most suitable candidate.

2 Use a panel of interviewers, perhaps from different parts of the organization.

3 Use an assessment center to weed out unsuitable candidates, and then interview only those who are above a certain baseline.

4 Ask candidates to complete a psychometric test,

and use the results as a basis for questions during a

panel interview.

5 Ask candidates to make a presentation, in conjunction

with a panel interview (especially if the candidate is

going to be the 'public face' of an organization).

MIX-AND-MATCH THE ABOVE APPROACHES
This chapter looks at how to negotiate some of the
other hurdles on the way to getting your next position.

The panel interview

An interview panel typically comprises the line manager for the position, someone from HR, a potential future colleague, a company director, and perhaps an outside appraiser.

All the advice given in Chapter 3 applies equally to a panel interview. However, there are further considerations to keep in mind when you are interacting with more than one person:

■ Listen very closely to any introductions. You could have to remember the names and positions of up to six people.

■ Position yourself so that you can make eye contact with all the panel members throughout the interview.

■ Listen carefully to the agenda.

■ Keep the entire panel in the conversation by maintaining eye contact with all of them, as well as the individual who has asked the question.

■ Never get drawn into an argument with a panel member, even if you disagree with what has been said. There may be an element of testing you by using this technique. If you feel this is the case don't be overly opinionated but be prepared to state your argument logically. If this does seem to be getting out of hand, don't panic. Use a phrase such as 'We should agree to differ on that point' and try, if possible, to get others on the panel to agree.

■ If there is a stiffness in the posture of a member of the panel, try to judge whether this was prompted by one of your responses, or whether this has been there since the start of the interview (this might indicate some internal tension within the interview panel).

■ Don't panic if members of the panel are not responding, but try to add some emphasis to the points you make to ensure that you are memorable to the panel.

■ Someone turning away is a negative sign. Either you are losing his or her attention, or you are rambling. If you are rambling, wrap up your point quickly; if you have lost someone, try hard with your next response to draw him or her back in.

■ Be aware if something you say causes a member of the panel to look again at your application or CV. Be prepared for a follow-up question to clarify an apparent mismatch between what you have said and what is in your written information.

in-depth interview scenarios

Common misconceptions about interview panels

There are several common misconceptions about interview panels.

THE PANEL MEMBERS HAVE READ YOUR CV

There is a good chance that the first time some of the panel members see your application or CV is when you walk into the interview room, and they might still be looking at the previous candidate's details, even then.

Assume the panel knows next to nothing about you. This is a benefit in one way as they may not have any preconceptions about you, and you can come to them with a clean slate.

THE PANEL MEMBERS ARE COMPETENT INTERVIEWERS

If you are lucky, at least one member of the panel will know how to ask questions to get the best out of you, but don't assume all are as skilful. You know your best selling points, the highs and lows of your career, the parts you want to emphasize, and those areas you want to gloss over. It's up to you to take control of the situation and guide the answers you give to the areas you want to showcase.

THE PANEL MEMBERS WANT TO BE THERE

In some cases, panel members are not there by choice. You might be going for a position in finance with a particular team, so a finance director from another part of the company may have been drafted in to check your credentials and acumen, but will have nothing to do with you, if you are hired, on a day-to-day basis. As far as that person is concerned, the interview is simply detracting from his or her normal workload.

You will have to work harder to draw these reluctant interviewers into the process. Be sure to ask relevant questions, perhaps about professional training or most desirable qualifications.

Assessment centres: an overview

The assessment centre is becoming increasingly popular with large and medium-sized organizations. There are a number of advantages for the organization in using them, not least is that the process is often run by professionals who take the full responsibility for meeting all legislative requirements for fair practice in selection.

The assessment centre may be used when an organization wants to employ a whole new team, as the methods used in this type of interview do indeed showcase different types of people and how they might work effectively as a unit.

Usually the process takes place over several days and may involve social events with potential colleagues in the evenings.

THE CONTENT MAY VARY BUT IT IS LIKELY TO INCLUDE:

1 Psychometric tests: this is a type of personality test.

2 Team-working exercise: this enables selectors to monitor performance in group situations.

3 In-box exercise: this will showcase individual organizational ability.

4 Presentations: these can be individual displays or form part of the team-working exercise.

5 Social events: these include working lunches, dinners or evening functions.

There are two major factors to remember about this type of interview:

■ You are on show the whole time, so beware of social gaffes.

■ Be yourself: it's difficult to keep up a persona that is not you over several days and in different business and social situations, with different groups of people.

in-depth interview scenarios

Meeting and greeting

This is when you will need to remember names and other details. Concentrate.

THERE ARE VARIOUS TRICKS TO NAME RECALL:

1 Associate some feature of the person with their name: 'Clare is wearing a blue blouse' or 'Doug is the guy with the beard'.

2 Repeat a name back when you introduce yourself: 'Hi Jason, I'm David'. This might help you to remember.

3 When you meet someone later in a one-on-one situation, ask that person to repeat his or her name. This suggests that the first meeting was rushed and you may be doing each other a favour.

Maintain a relaxed posture. This might be difficult if you are nervous, but you should try taking a few deep breaths before entering a room. Make eye contact with the people to whom you are introduced and offer a warm handshake to everyone present.

Keep in mind the preparation you have undertaken. This will help you feel more confident. If you have done your homework on the organization, you should not feel out of place.

Be confident in your approach to the people to whom you are introduced. This is also the time to be listening to glean any further information on the organization and the people who will be involved in your interview. The composition of the selection team can offer valuable clues as to the types of people who might fit the profile.

Listen carefully to instructions about venues, moving around and so on.

Psychometric testing

A type of personality test, psychometric testing points out various personality traits and can be a useful basis for questions in your interview.

In a psychometric test, you answer several questions. The answers you give can provide clues – and only clues – to your personality. These tests are indicative of an individual's personality, no more. You should be told at the start of the process – and it is true – that there are no 'right' or 'wrong' answers. All the answers in this type of test are unique to you.

These tests are scored or rated into general 'fields' or types of behaviour. The scoring gives clues to personality type and profile and can help to pinpoint personal behavioural styles. These styles or characteristics will be analyzed and then passed on to the selection panel.

These results will not be used to make the decision on your suitability for a position, but they are likely to influence the areas in which the panel will focus questions. For example, if the personality profile you show is for strong leadership, you may be asked about leadership situations and your ability to follow instructions. Psychometric testing shows strengths and weaknesses.

Tests tend to take the form of a number of multiple-choice questions that pose situations or ask about your feelings toward events. They may appear quite random in nature, but this is part of the internal check mechanism of the process to attempt to make the responses as truthful as possible.

Normally the questions are set against a time limit to ensure that you give instinctive answers and do not have time to go back through the paper trying to second guess the answers to change your profile.

It is best to approach the test in an open, confident manner. You cannot change the person you are, and trying to 'cheat' is not going to get you a job you want, even if you get an offer. Test papers are devised with internal checks to ensure consistency, so trying to fool the tester is not a good idea. It is also worth bearing in mind that this a snapshot of you on that day at that time, and many interviewers will want to get beyond the individual test results and see the real you.

You should be given the chance to see and discuss the outcome of the testing with the qualified person who has organized the test (who will usually be acting independently from the interview process). Always ask for this feedback. Questions asked in the panel stage of the interview process will be based on your psychometric profile, and this will help you to prepare for them.

Effective in-box exercises

An in-box exercise, as the name suggests, presents you with a stack of paper of varying degrees of importance and asks you to work through it.

THE IN-BOX EXERCISE IS OFTEN USED IN LARGE CORPORATIONS AS A TOOL FOR ASSESSING HOW ABLE INTERVIEW CANDIDATES ARE AT:

1 Organizing themselves

2 Organizing those who work for them

3 Seeing the big picture

They also give the interviewer more information about you. They are your chance to show that you can work effectively.

You likely do 'in-box exercises' in your job anyway, so don't panic if you are told that this is part of the interview process. Nonetheless, remember that the planning and prioritizing you do in real life will be watched and assessed during the interview. The exercise will be timed and is likely to be set up in such a way as to appear to give you a lot to do in a short time, but there are probably going to be one or two major items that need your attention among many minor tasks that are there to confuse. Yes, it is exactly like any day in the office.

You need to get organized. If you need more space, spread out the contents of the in-box so that you can see it all before you start working on any one item. Remember that the exercise is about prioritizing, not about shuffling paper.

You know from your career so far that quite often at work the most important or significant items don't stand out, so take the time to scan through all the items in the in-box to establish their relative priority.

Mark them A, B, C, etc., with a pile for each. Work on the ones that need urgent action (As); decide early on what can be delegated and mark these, providing a timeframe for someone to do those. In other words, manage the flow of information. Work on the A priorities and demonstrate your grasp of the problems in them – this is the work that will score you the points.

in-depth interview scenarios

Team-building exercises

Few jobs exist in isolation. The vast majority involve working as part of a team, even if you are heading it up. For this reason, a selection procedure might involve a team-building exercise.

There are various styles of team-building exercises, and they can vary considerably in the number of people involved at any one time.

The simplest are like extensions of the in-box exercise in which you and a group of fellow candidates are asked to work through information to reach a conclusion or produce a report.

The most complex might involve information being provided by computer and updated by emails or other reports as the exercise progresses. Part of your task will be to respond to this information.

However simple or complex the exercise, the underlying principles are the same – to establish how you and your fellow candidates work as a team and in teams. To do well, you need to be aware of the basic principles of working in teams or groups.

TEAM MEMBERS

There are a number of ways of looking at team members and the roles people take when working together. Broadly speaking, they split into groups 1 to 5 listed on the page opposite. The 4 points listed on pages 158 to 159 will also help you in team-building exercises.

1 Leaders of various types

2 Followers or co-workers

3 New ideas people

4 Outcome checkers

5 Investigators of resources

PLAY TO YOUR STRENGTHS

It may sound obvious, but you need to know your own characteristics and be able to play to the strength of each one of them.

Don't try to be someone you are not, but do build on the best ways of working for you.

Always keep in mind that this is a competition. Although you need to be able to show team spirit because this is what is being tested, you also need your good qualities to shine.

TEAM RELATIONSHIPS

You should keep an open mind with a team exercise. For example, an exercise may have been set up with a designated leader, but that person may not be the natural leader in the group. All of your actions will be scrutinized so you need to think carefully about interjecting into a flow of discussion. Always listen more than you speak. Use reflection of the discussion to move it forward to other areas. This is a management exercise, so manage the group, even if you are not the designated leader.

BE AWARE OF THE REST OF THE TEAM

You definitely want your qualities to be noticed, but there is a lot to be gained by being the group member who moves the team forward. If you can refer to statements made by others that have somehow gotten lost in the discussion and establish some sort of consensus, you will score points for being able to draw the threads of discussion together. You might well defuse tension or conflict by doing this and move everyone forward.

UNDERSTAND THE UNDERLYING PRINCIPLE

Try to figure out why you are being asked to take part in this type of exercise. Is it because the interviewers are genuinely looking to appoint a team? Or is it to see how different candidates react in managerial and subordinate situations? Second guessing can be tricky, but it may help your candidacy if you know that what is required is someone who can collaborate successfully with many different people, for example, or someone who can be an incisive leader.

160

'Trial by orange juice'

An assessment centre interview is almost certain to involve food and drink at some point.

You are on show and you will be judged on your ability to eat while conversing, have a responsible attitude towards alcohol and not spill anything on your clothes. Having said that, social events are a great time to gather more information about the position, the company and even the interview panel, as well as the other candidates. They also allow you to show that you are a well-rounded, interesting individual, who could bring a unique blend of skills and talents to the organization.

SOME BASIC RULES:

1 Don't be indiscreet about the process so far. You may be talking to the person who devised it.

2 Do more listening than talking, be reflective and active in your listening and wait for the gaps in the flow of conversation to make your points.

3 Even if you've established a genuine rapport with the person sitting next to you, be a social butterfly. You want to demonstrate your ease with all sorts of people.

4 Manage your nerves any way you can, except by using alcohol or tobacco.

5 Avoid sauces (which can drip on that crisp white shirt), highly spiced foods (you may not smell it on your breath but others can), and food that is labour intensive like lobster, so you can concentrate on what's being said around you.

6 Don't overfill your plate or revisit the dessert cart – if nerves make you want to eat, pack an emergency snack in your suitcase and eat it in your room later. The best line is moderation in everything.

in-depth interview scenarios
Presentations: an overview

At some stage in the interview process you may be asked to make some form of presentation. This might be:

1 An informal presentation to the interview panel of three or four people.

2 A critique of one of the company's products or services.

3 A formal presentation to the company's senior executives.

4 A talk to a group of outsiders such as a friends organization (more likely if you are applying to a hospital, charity, arts or academic institution).

You might also be asked to lead a training session, seminar or to set up a mock press conference. All these scenarios are designed to test you: remember, such skills can be acquired through practice.

Whatever the size of the audience or the length and complexity of the presentation, the same basic principles apply.

1 Do your research.

2 Prepare what you are going to say.

3 Rehearse it until you know it perfectly.

4 Practice to make sure it sounds spontaneous.

5 Enjoy yourself. If you can't do it in an interview situation, you are not likely to be able to do it in a real one, so consider whether you really are trying for the right position.

What a presentation says about you

During the interview process you are in the business of marketing yourself and a presentation should be all about selling your uniqueness.

THIS IS YOUR OPPORTUNITY TO SHOW:

1 What you know.

2 That you can develop a convincing argument.

3 That you are an effective communicator.

This really is a golden opportunity for you, so grab it with both hands, work at producing a good presentation and practice presenting it effectively.

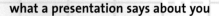
A presentation is a test of your ability to explain complex issues to show how you can think through the problems that face an organization and come up with results. The good news is that you will have time to prepare in advance.

The actual presentation gives you the opportunity to show how you can keep a group interested and is a practical chance for you to demonstrate leadership skills. To take that opportunity, you need to be prepared and to have worked out well in advance what you are going to say.

in-depth interview scenarios

Preparing the presentation

Planning is everything when it comes to making a presentation. You have the advantage of being able to take your time, collect all the information you need and put together a good package.

ESTABLISH AS CLEARLY AS YOU CAN WHAT THE PRESENTATION IS ABOUT:

1 What issues do you need to address?

2 What areas of the business are you to review?

3 What information will you be expected to present and what will the audience already know?

4 How much detail will you be expected to supply?

5 How long is the presentation expected to be?

6 To whom will you be making your presentation?

HAVING ESTABLISHED THESE BASIC FACTS, YOU WILL BE ABLE TO PLAN OUT WHAT YOU WANT TO SAY AND THINK ABOUT THE BEST WAYS TO GET YOUR MESSAGE ACROSS LOGICALLY.

1 How will you develop your arguments?

2 Do you need statistical analysis to back up what you want to say?

3 Are you going to quote other researchers, rely on your own experience or mix and match the two approaches?

Develop a series of main headings, for example:

IN A FINANCIAL REPORT:

1 Last year's quarterly figures

2 Industry averages

3 Your projections for the company

4 Actions you propose for moving between present and projection

IN A HUMAN RESOURCES PRESENTATION:

1 Company turnover statistics

2 Your analysis

3 A proposal for exit questionnaires

4 Examples of how these have helped other organizations

5 How you would implement strategy

These points will form the basis of your notes to act as prompts during the presentation. There is nothing worse than someone reading the script of a presentation – it won't get your message across, no matter how good the material.

Put the main points of the presentation on cards that you can keep with you to aid recall. These may also form the basis of your visual aids.

Think about whether you need to use visual aids, and, if so, how, what and when. Can you produce them yourself? Will the venue have all the necessary equipment you might need?

THESE ARE SOME OF THE VISUAL AIDS YOU MIGHT USE:

1 A flip chart of paper: this is the simplest visual aid you can use. It allows you to clearly write the main points of your presentation. If you want to use this method, buy a suitably sized pad, write up the main points in advance and reveal them as you go along.

2 Poster-style charts: these can be displayed and revealed to demonstrate the main points in your presentation. This is particularly useful when using graphs or charts to give financial or statistical information. Again, you can prepare it all in advance.

3 Overhead projector slides: these can also be produced ahead of time. You can place images, graphs, charts and written material in the same slides, which is a definite advantage.

4 Computer-based programs: these types of presentations are becoming increasingly popular and are easily available, but your audience may have seen the standard presentation in some programmes numerous times already. If you are going down this route, produce something original, possibly using the logo and colours of the organization to which you are talking.

Spelling and grammar of any presentation material must be faultless. If in doubt, get a friend you trust to check over the presentation for any errors.

PRACTICE MAKES PERFECT
You wrote the presentation and you own it. All you need to do now is demonstrate this. Get enthusiastic about it, and practice, practice and practice. Ideally, do it in front of different audiences – male/female is an obvious split, young/old might work, as might corporate/ academic friends. Watch who you lose and who understands what you've done. Modify, as necessary.

in-depth interview scenarios

Checklist: before the day

CALL TO CHECK THAT EVERYTHING IS READY FOR YOU. THE BASICS INCLUDE:

1 Where will you give the presentation?

Where are the building and room located?

2 What time are you expected to start?

When can you set up?

3 Check that the equipment you need is in the room or will be available. If you are working with computer technology, you need to make sure that you have the correct cables to use with projectors.

4 It is worth checking out the room in advance in case

it is larger than you expect. The size of the

typeface on your visual aids may need to be adjusted.

5 Ensure you know how many people will be in

your audience, particularly if you intend to have hand outs.

You need to have enough copies.

6 If you can specify the layout of the seating in

advance, you have the chance to organize the room

to your best advantage.

CHECKLIST

The presentation itself

Make sure you have analyzed the subject matter and collected the relevant data. You want to make yourself familiar with the subject being presented. You will need to be passionate to make the presentation effective.

Organize the presentation in a logical way:

■ Prepare an opener that sets the scene for your audience.

■ Give an indication early on of the content and duration of the presentation, and explain the type of visual aids you're going to use. There is nothing worse than asking your audience to turn around to look at a screen, especially if they haven't been expecting to move.

■ If you ask a question at the beginning of the presentation, answer it at the end, after having presented the information to back up your answer.

■ Don't immediately give the answer to the question you ask at the beginning: wait until you have set out the facts.

■ You are selling yourself so be prepared to use your information to demonstrate your own understanding of the subject.

■ A presentation will also be an opportunity for you to show that you have researched the organization (see Chapter 1, page 11); most people like to have their previous successes mentioned so be positive about the good things you have found.

■ Stick to the subject, rolling out a logical flow of information.

TIMING

It is very important to know how long your presentation is expected to be. You will need to practice it to check the timing. If you have been asked to present for 10 minutes make sure it is about 8 minutes long and then invite questions.

You also need to consider how many visual aids you can use in the time allocated. As a general rule, you want no more than one slide or page of information every two minutes.

So in a ten-minute presentation, you need to ask your audience to absorb no more than 5 slides, posters or pages of a computer presentation. Don't bombard your audience with information: a few well-chosen facts and images are far more effective.

Too short is as bad as too long. Running through your whole presentation several times will help you guarantee that you do not run out of steam early and are able to meet the allotted time limits.

Making the presentation

You have everything prepared and ready; all you have to do is speak. Make sure:

- You have checked the room.

- You arrive on time.

- You have all the necessary materials for your presentation.

You need to use any nervous energy to your best advantage and sell yourself. You have been asked to make a presentation so that the panel can find out whether:

- You have a big presence.

- You are timid or extrovert.

- You can hold an audience.

- You can explain complex issues in simple terms.

When you are presenting:

- Always stand: you want to give the impression of authority, which will add impact to anything you say.

- If you need to hold notes, use index cards, which are easy to hold.

- Put a tag or rubber band through a hole in the corner of the cards so they stay in order if you drop them.

- Avoid waving your arms about, but don't stand with your hands in your pockets either.

- Assume a relaxed easy posture with shoulders down and feet slightly apart.

- Don't stand rooted to the spot. A little movement, perhaps to point at something on screen is a good way of showing your confidence and ownership of both the space and subject matter.

- Speak clearly and audibly but don't shout. Your voice is important.

- Keep the volume up and add some inflection and different tone to ensure interest.

- Use a short pause before starting to ensure that you have the full attention of your audience.

in-depth interview scenarios

Your task now is to deliver your message clearly. To do so:

1 Speak to all the people in the room.

2 Don't talk to the ceiling.

3 Don't talk to the visual aids.

4 Don't talk to the tops of the chairs.

5 Don't talk to the spaces between the chairs.

Make your presentation to all the room. For large groups, make sure you slowly sweep the room with your gaze.

Show some passion for the subject. Think of it as an audition for a part you were born to play.

Finally, smile and enjoy it.

INVITING AND ANSWERING
QUESTIONS:

As you start your presentation,
it is a good idea to set out the
length of the presentation and
to determine when you will take
and answer questions. It is
probably best to take the
questions at the end of the
presentation; otherwise, they may
break up your flow. Keep answers
brief and to the point so that as
many people as possible who
want to ask a question get the
opportunity to do so.

ANSWERING DIFFICULT
QUESTIONS:

■ As with the interview itself,
don't answer questions if you
don't understand them. Ask
for clarification.

■ Always refer back to the
information you have given in
the presentation as the
evidence for your answer.

■ Don't get into an argument. If
you do find someone who
disagrees with your
information or interpretation
just 'agree
to differ'.

Checklist: presentations

1 Clearly agree on the subject.

2 Establish the target audience.

3 Agree on the length of the presentation.

4 Research your subject.

5 Choose your information.

6 Decide on the main points you wish to make.

7 Choose the type of visual aids you will use.

8 Practice with your visual aids.

9 Reduce presentation contents to index cards.

10 Check the venue.

CHECKLIST

5

accepting an offer

Evaluating an offer

The offer of a job that you worked hard to secure is the start of a whole new process – evaluating the position and its starting package and deciding if it really is right for you at this time.

At more senior levels, you are likely to target potential vacancies, do serious research before you even put in an application and know from the interview whether you want the position or not. However, there are occasions when you might be in the position of having to evaluate more than one offer at the same time:

- You have to evaluate any job offer against your current position.

- Because your CV is with more than one recruitment consultant, you'll likely have the opportunity for several interviews.

- Successful networking secures you an interview at the same time as you put in an application for a position.

All the information and advice given in this chapter on looking at offers and negotiating packages applies regardless of how many offers you are evaluating simultaneously.

When you get a job offer, ask for time to consider it, but be sure to specify when you will respond. Before you say yes, you need to do some serious thinking.

YOUR CHECKLIST

Look again at:

■ Your list of skills

■ Your USP (Unique Selling Proposition)

■ Your career goals (both short and medium term)

■ Your bottom line in terms of what you are looking for in your career, now and in the future

■ Your research on the company

The background work you did got you the offer, but look again at all the information, and think about what was said at the interview.

■ Does your reading of the company match its reading of itself, gained from the interview?

■ Does your reading of industry trends match the company's?

■ Energy and enthusiasm from potential colleagues are good signs if they are backed up by results – profitability or expansion, for example.

■ Change is usually perceived as 'good', a force that motivates people, keeps them fresh, and improves organizational cultures. If you are coming from this mindset, taking a new job is a good move. But there are further things to keep in mind.

Is it right for me?

Timing is important in career terms: The right job at the wrong time can be as harmful as taking the wrong job. In addition to considering salary and other benefits, you need to decide whether this move is a good one at this time.

LIFESTYLE

If you are single, most positions are acceptable. If you have family commitments, however, you must consider your family in any move. For example, the position you are pursuing will involve at least a couple of nights away from home each week, or perhaps periods 'on the road' or several trade fairs or conferences each year.

1 Are you prepared not to see your children every day?

2 Will you miss parent–teacher reviews?

Older children will probably be happy with a call or email each evening, but being away from home can be difficult if your children are small and will place extra work on your partner.

ACCLIMATIZATION

A new job means an enormous time commitment in getting up to speed, adapting to a new organization and new colleagues, and generally fitting in.

In addition, you have to consider whether you will spend more time commuting. The working week is not only about the hours you spend at work.

1 Can you free up the time you need to spend in the office, over and above an 'average' working week?

2 Are you prepared to put projects on hold for the time being?

CAREER STATUS
Think about where you are and where you want to be, in one year,
in three years, in five years.

1 Is this position a means to an end or is it an end in itself?

2 Does it offer the on-the-job training you really need?

3 Can you 'see' your next move, if you take on this position now?

ORGANIZATION
Moving from a small company to a large one or vice versa can be a culture
shock, so think carefully if this move involves such a transition.

1 Do you want the challenge of really counting in an organization?

2 Are you prepared to be a small cog in a large wheel?

3 Did you get a good sense of teamwork and team building? Is there a commitment to staff development?

4 Can you grow with this company?

THE POSITION
A job with built-in obsolescence, for example closing a facility, may mean that it will not be long before you are job seeking again.

1 Is this right for you now?

2 Do you need a settled income and a settled position for a couple of years while you get established in your new environment?

Checklist: making a decision

Draw up a simple list of all the issues you can think of and check them off:

LIFESTYLE

1 No major impact on time at home ☐

Will involve family change ☐

Thought about and discussed all issues ☐

CAREER STATUS

2 Move in the right direction ☐

Could be perceived as a lateral move,
but interesting ☐

Next move could be... ☐

Good to have on my CV ☐

ORGANIZATION

3 Financially stable ☐

Worth taking a chance ☐

Good record on staff development ☐

Good record on staff retention ☐

Commitment to training ☐

POSITION

4 Open ended ☐

Fixed term ☐

CHECKLIST

Relocation issues

It might be a good job, and have come at just the right time. More importantly, your family is behind you, but relocation should never be undertaken lightly.

NATIONAL/INTERNATIONAL CONSIDERATIONS

- Are you going to sell a home and buy a new one?

- Will you rent out your current home with a view to returning some day?

- Do you need to store any furniture or belongings?

- Will you need to ship your goods overseas?

- Is there a company culture that helps employees relocate, or are you going to have to do all the hard work yourself?

- What are the timing issues? Do you have to be settled before you start work, or can you spend time in a hotel or commuting on a week-by-week basis until you are all in your new home?

- Are you ready to live in the city/the mountains/the country or will you miss fast food/peace and quiet/clean air?

SCHOOLS

■ If you have children, can you get help and advice on suitable schools where you are going?

■ If you are relocating abroad, are there language issues? Will your children have to be in a class with younger children because their language skills are not up to standard? (Generally, the younger your children are, the easier they will adapt.)

■ Are there financial implications around schooling decisions?

PARTNERS

■ Is your partner going to be able to find work?

■ Does your partner have the necessary permits to work where you are going?

■ If a career break is a good option, have you considered the financial implications?

■ Are there good study opportunities where you are going?

Negotiating a starting package

After you have the offer and you have decided that you want the position, you need to consider what conditions will make you accept. Remember that the package you negotiate at this point is one that you will have to live with for some time; once you have accepted it and are actually doing the job, your ability to change anything basic is lost.

You probably have a good knowledge of the salary rates across your industry, and where your experience places you in the salary range. Your professional body can also offer advice and information, but you should also look at recruitment consultants' web sites for salary ranges in similar positions. If you are changing direction or are new to an industry, be realistic about what you are bringing. You might have to compromise on salary to make up for greater job satisfaction or more security, for example.

Consider what items will make or break a deal. You might need to think about the items from your own lifestyle that you are willing to compromise on. You may be able to accept changes to meet the needs of your potential new employer (longer hours or more travelling, for example), but you want to get sufficient compensation for the changes, either in the form of basic salary or as additional benefits.

Always think of the whole package, rather than only the salary. For example, any training that the company will pay for can save you thousands of dollars; it might be worth taking a lower salary as a trade-off against free or subsidized training.

Paid holiday time should also be part of the package. If you have been with an employer for some time, you may have earned extra days off. With a new employer, you might have to accept the basic holiday package.

So before you enter into any negotiation, establish clearly in your own mind the items you will not compromise on and that are nonnegotiable, and those areas that are open to negotiation and compromise.

Negotiation is a two-way process

Negotiation is about getting a dialogue going. Remember that, at this point, both you and your future employer are committed to same thing – getting you on board to the satisfaction of all parties.

You are trying to get to a 'win-win' position – that is, a point at which both you and the organization have gained the maximum benefit from the process. They have your full commitment to the position: You are prepared to put in the hours required above and beyond the norm, you are prepared to travel as required, and so on. You have the salary you require, and you have the level of benefits that complete the package.

The key to effective negotiation is communication. You let them know what you want and why. Remember that you can always agree to come down from what you are asking for, but it is difficult to get an employer to shift upward once you have said what you want. Consider the underlying value of every part of an offer; do not look at the salary alone. A lower salary may be acceptable if an employer contributes to a pension plan, for example; a car may be added to your salary for tax purposes, so it may not be the great deal it seems, especially if it is used as a means to justify a low salary offer.

The process is likely to go back and forth, with offer and counteroffer. Always ask to consider an offer, even if you think it is a good one. This shows that you are taking the process seriously and are eager to get the package right.

GETTING HELP

If you are uncomfortable about negotiating or think that you will not get the best deals you could, consider career counselling in this area. Consultants run one-on-one sessions or day seminars specifically on this, as well as other, career issues. You may wish to work with a qualified career counsellor on an open-ended basis, to facilitate the acclimation process as you settle into your new position.

negotiating benefits

The salary is never the bottom line in any remunerations package you negotiate. Consider other benefits and individual perquisites as part of your negotiations.

TRAINING

Any training you are getting for free, or at a reduced rate, is an important consideration, especially if you would have to pay for it in another company. Remember that time has cost implications, too.

1 Are you drawing a salary when you attend training days?

2 Are you being paid when you are studying?

CAR ALLOWANCES AND TRAVEL

If you have to travel for the position, car allowances and travel reimbursements will be an important consideration.

1 Will you have some sort of car allowance?

2 Will you have travel refunded? If so, how and when?

3 If overnight stays are involved, how will the costs be met?

HEALTHCARE

Healthcare is obviously very important, but it may be one of the more important elements of your remuneration package, depending upon your age and family circumstances.

1 What sort of healthcare coverage does the company offer as a standard part of the contract?

2 How much additional coverage are they willing to offer?

3 Does the company scheme cover your family?

ENTERTAINING CLIENTS

If there is a lot of entertaining of potential and existing clients, you need to understand the company's policy on meeting expenses.

1 How and when will expenses be refunded?

You are in a better position financially if you have a company credit or charge card for all your business expenses than if you have to pay for, and then reclaim, expenses every month.

MATERNITY AND PATERNITY LEAVE

For many people, not getting enough time to stay home with a new baby is a real and important issue. Paid leave varies widely, with some companies only offering the legal minimum. You might consider that a lower salary but a longer period of paid maternity or paternity leave is a good trade-off.

1 What are the employer's family leave provisions?

2 Is there childcare on site?

OTHER AREAS
Think too about 'intangibles', factors that might be important to you but that do not really carry a price tag. Consider areas such as:

1 Flexible working hours (to be home in time to bathe the children or to fit in a session at the gym).

2 Flexible holiday arrangements (especially if other family members have to take holidays at fixed periods: will you have the flexibility to join them?).

3 Ability to work at home some days.

Checklist: negotiations

CURRENT POSITION

1
Salary _____
Bonuses _____
Commissions _____
Paid holiday _____
Annual take-home pay _____

BENEFITS

2
Healthcare ☐

Dental ☐

Life insurance ☐

Severance pay ☐

Car ☐

Pension ☐

Training ☐

Other ☐

PERQUISITES

3
Expense account ☐

Office ☐

Laptop computer ☐

Mobile expenses ☐

Clothing allowance ☐

Paid personal holidays ☐

Membership dues, meeting fees ☐

Transportation costs ☐

NEW POSITION

1
Salary _____
Bonuses _____
Commissions _____
Paid holiday _____
Annual take-home pay _____

BENEFITS

2
Healthcare ☐
Dental ☐
Life insurance ☐
Severance pay ☐
Car ☐
Pension ☐
Training ☐
Other ☐

PERQUISITES

3
Expense account ☐
Office ☐
Laptop computer ☐
Mobile expenses ☐
Clothing allowance ☐
Paid personal holidays ☐
Membership dues, meeting fees ☐
Transportation costs ☐

CHECKLIST

Accepting the offer

When the negotiations are complete and you have accepted the offer, there are still a few details to be ironed out before you can formally accept an offer and hand in your notice to your current employer.

When you have reached agreement on a remuneration package, you still need to discuss:

1 Start date

2 Notice period

3 Contract

WHEN TO START

You are likely to need a start date so that a contract of employment can be drawn up by the organization. If you are on a standard notice period that you are unable to negotiate, it is easy to work out when you can start. Consider, however, whether you might want a break before you take on a new challenge. Do you want to rest a week or two to mentally and physically remove yourself from the old job, or are you eager to get on with the new one?

Whatever you decide, starting on the first of the month is often a good idea administratively, as is starting after a public holiday or on the first day of a new term.

MEETING THE TEAM

Depending on how the interview was conducted, and with whom, you might want to suggest a 'meet the team' session before you officially start, or find out if there are any social events or training sessions you could take part in. This is a good way of breaking the ice before taking up a new position. Alternatively, some companies will hold orientation or induction sessions for new staff members. If this is not offered, you could request it.

RELOCATION

If you are moving to a new city, confirm what arrangements are in place to help you relocate, and build in time to plan and carry out your move.

Keep in mind factors such as changing schools; if you have children it may be easier for them to start at the beginning of a new semester.

Also remember that moving is both physically and emotionally draining. Do not underestimate the time and volume of paperwork involved.

When your employer wants you to stay

Handing in your notice may make your existing employer review your current position or your remuneration package, or both. Think hard before responding.

1 Never reject an overture to improve your current status. Always ask for time to consider.

2 You almost certainly are not considering a move simply for status or financial gain. A move now is part of your overall career strategy. Do you want to be deflected?

3 Do you believe that your overall contribution is indeed valued, or is your current employer simply panicking at the thought of replacing you?

4 In many positions, it is the people around you, or your boss's support, that make the difference between a happy company and a frustrating one. However, people change and move on. The status quo may not be the status quo in six-months' time, and you might have wasted a golden opportunity.

5 If your current employer can match what you have secured elsewhere, why didn't they do so earlier?

6 Change is refreshing and invigorating. Yes, it can be hard work, but nothing really worth achieving is easy.

7 Staying in your 'comfort zone' is understandable, but remember all the effort you have put into securing the new position.

8 Part of your deliberations was likely the effect a move would have on your CV. Do you really need another year in this position to make you more marketable?

9 Before you reject the potential new employer, get the terms of a new deal with your current employer in writing, with review dates for potential follow-up.

Exit strategies

The key to leaving a company is to act at all times with consummate professionalism, doing your job to the best of your ability until the day you have agreed to leave.

Never resign until you have signed and returned a contract of employment (or at least a letter of agreement) from your new employer. Keep your letter of resignation short and focused.

NOTICE PERIODS

If you are doing consulting or freelance work, you will have to judge how much notice you give; an employer deserves time to find someone to fill your role (you might even suggest someone suitable). Otherwise, your contract of employment will specify a period of notice.

■ A fixed, nonnegotiable period, such as one month or three months, or in academic establishments, more likely a term or semester

■ A 'clear-your-desk now' period

If you are on a fixed period, consider whether you want to try to negotiate down. For example, if business is slack, an employer might release you early to cut the staff bill. Some employers would rather release you early than risk you starting to affect the morale of those around you.

CONFIDENTIALITY ISSUES

In any organization, there are going to be confidentiality issues to think about while you work out your notice and after you have left. You must be scrupulous about what you take with you. If you do have to work out a lengthy notice period, ask your current employer if you can take a back seat in any negotiations that could be construed as a potential conflict of interest. Ask how you should handle telling clients and suppliers that you are leaving. Your employer might want you to wait until your successor has been found so that you can say, 'And effective from Monday 12/3, your contact will be...', or to ask your clients to deal with your replacement directly during your notice period.

IT'S A SMALL WORLD

Mentally you might be thinking 'I would never work for X again', but people do bump into each other down the line. So 'never say never', and don't burn any bridges. Remember, too, that the entire workforce is more mobile than it was even 20 years ago. People who stay with one company are the exception, and those who do will have a series of different jobs within it.

PERSONAL ISSUES

How far you want to go verbally is up to you. It may be that you want to tell your line manager something of your real reasons for leaving, but it is generally wisest to stick to something like 'a new challenge'.

accepting an offer

Your notice period

A period of notice is a breathing space, allowing you to ease yourself out of your current position and mentally gear up for the challenge of your new one.

APPROACH YOUR NOTICE PERIOD AS A SCHEDULE FOR DEPARTURE. PLAN OUT WITH YOUR MANAGER WHAT NEEDS TO BE:

1 Finished by you

2 Allocated to someone else

THEN, CREATE A TIMEFRAME TO COMPLETE THE WORK.

FELLOW WORKERS

The people you work with on a daily basis are likely to be pleased that you have a new challenge. Keep your relationships with them as professional as possible.

HANDOVER

Most organizations will be concerned to make sure there is a smooth handover of any work to be monitored or completed after you leave. Giving this attention will pay dividends. You want your current employer to be sorry to lose a professional employee who effected a smooth transition.

Make sure all files are up to date, any email correspondence is forwarded to whichever team member is taking over your projects, and most loose ends are taken care of in good time.

Schedule a meeting during your last week to be sure everyone who needs to know the status of your projects is clear on where to find everything.

CONFIDENTIALITY CLAUSES

You may be asked to sign a confidentiality statement preventing you from taking any work with particular clients or in a field of activity that may be classed as competition. Here it is best to keep your future employer in the loop to ensure that you are not compromising yourself. You cannot be forced to sign a retrospective confidentiality clause if it was not part of your original terms of employment.

FUTURE CONTACT

As a gesture of goodwill, leave a phone number or email address where you can be contacted if necessary. You do not want your first days and weeks in a new position to be filled with calls from your previous employer. On the other hand, if something really has gone astray, you will want to help former colleagues locate it. Your home email might be a good address to leave.

The exit interview with HR

Exit interviews are conducted with departing employees, just before they leave. From the employer's perspective, the primary aim of the exit interview is to learn reasons for the person's departure and to understand these to achieve organizational improvement.

Good exit interviews should provide useful information about the employer organization, to assess and improve all aspects of the working environment, culture, processes and systems, management and development – in short, anything that contributes to the quality of the organization.

An exit interview is a chance for you to give some constructive feedback and to leave on a positive note, with good relations and mutual respect. Resist the temptation for recrimination, blame, revenge and spite. Be calm, fair, objective and as helpful as possible. The business world is relatively small, and you may cross the paths of your former colleagues and managers in the future.

The exit interview will usually be conducted face-to-face because this enables better communication, understanding, and interpretation. From the HR professional's viewpoint, it provides a far better opportunity to probe and get to the root of sensitive subjects. However, postal or electronic questionnaires may be the norm in your organization.

THESE ARE SOME TYPICAL QUESTIONS YOU MAY BE ASKED AT THE EXIT INTERVIEW.

■ Tell me about how you've come to decide to leave?

■ What is your main reason for leaving?

■ How do you feel about this organization?

■ What has been good/ enjoyable/satisfying for you in your time with us?

■ How could the organization have enabled you to make fuller use of your capabilities and potential?

■ How would you describe the culture of this organization?

■ What can you say about the way your performance was measured, and the feedback to you of your performance results?

■ What would you say about how you were motivated? How could that have been improved?

■ How can the organization gather and make better use of the views and experience of all its employees?

■ Would you consider working again for us if the situation were right?

Checklist: starting a new job

The first days and weeks in a new job are a period of adjustment on all sides. Your manager and the rest of the team are getting used to you and your methods of working, and you are getting used to the way the organization works. There are ways to make this adjustment process easier.

1 Be clear what you need to bring on day one. For example, you may need bank details so your salary is paid or a photo for your ID card.

2 Establish whether there is to be a formal induction meeting, and when and where it will be held.

3 For the first few weeks, arrive early and stay until a task is finished.

4 Find out about regular meetings/briefings/updates.

ESTABLISH WITH YOUR LINE MANAGER WHEN THE TWO OF YOU MEET:

1 Be clear about areas where you can act with autonomy and what needs to be reported immediately.

2 Get your goals for the first month, and then the next five months, established and agreed.

3 Schedule any trips, trade shows, fairs or conferences.

4 Show initiative and willingness to learn.

5 Get yourself on mailing and circulation lists.

6 Take up any social opportunities.

CHECKLIST

career management

After an unsuccessful interview

Qualifications and experience are only one ingredient in the 'fit' of candidate to role. Chemistry, timing and potential are others. Interviews that do not produce the desired outcome are not necessarily unsuccessful.

TAKING POSITIVES FROM EVERY INTERVIEW:

1 Each interview gives you more practice for future interviews.

2 Every conversation you have with someone who works in your industry gives you an insight into problems and opportunities.

3 Take every interview opportunity to build up a better understanding of yourself and your strengths and weaknesses.

4 From every interview you should be able to take away additional skills that you can use the next time.

5 Each interview is different, but there will be common threads that you can review to give you a better performance next time.

6 Some of your answers will have been good. You need to analyze the interview and identify the best ones for future use.

7 Erase words such as 'rejection' from your vocabulary.

8 Acknowledge that if it didn't work out in the interview, it is unlikely that it would have worked out had you got the job.

Why feedback is important

Getting feedback on your performance at the interview is useful for every future interview you attend. Ideally, the process begins immediately after you exit the interview room as you review every question you were asked, statement you made and the comments that everyone involved made.

Getting an interview is a good sign that your skills and experience were about right for the job offered, but if you didn't get the position and, especially, if this happens two or three times, you need to find out if there is a problem. Feedback from a line manager and others involved in the interview will help you to:

■ Identify whether there is a contradiction between what's on your CV and what you have actually done in your career. For example, is your CV inflating the roles and experience you have had?

■ Decide whether you are applying for the wrong type of positions.

■ Pinpoint whether you are applying to the wrong sorts of companies.

■ Find any deficiencies in your interview skills.

■ Point out training and development needs.

■ Identify appropriate behaviour for the next interview.

■ Focus on your core strengths and get these across in any future interview.

■ Draw a line under this interview and approach the next one with a positive frame of mind.

Some of these factors you will probably have identified yourself (see pp. 134–137), but it's always useful to have the independent view of an industry professional. Interviewers are in a position to offer an objective view of your performance.

Listening and talking

You may need to be persistent to elicit feedback on your performance. However, take every opportunity to gain an insight into why your candidacy did not secure an offer on this occasion.

Some organizations do not contact unsuccessful interviewees, but usually you will get a call, email or letter from the line manager or from HR to let you know that, on this occasion, your application has been unsuccessful. This is the time to get out the list you made after the interview (see pp. 134–137) and ask for feedback on your performance. This is a perfectly reasonable request, especially if you thought you were a good fit, although many organizations may not routinely offer this service.

If you have written to everyone who interviewed you, you have a greater chance of eliciting candid information and valuable insights from one or more of them.

Some of the factors you identified are likely to be offered as reasons you were unsuccessful on this occasion; others may not. After you have listened to what is said, don't be afraid to ask searching questions of your own.

Make questions as open as you can to elicit useful information, and start with the ones that relate specifically to you rather than to the other candidates.

1 What was the biggest factor in my interview that led you to offer the position to someone else?

2 Are there any areas where you felt my skills were not up to the job?

3 Did you identify any training needs I should address?

FUTURE OPPORTUNITIES

It is always worth asking if you can be kept in mind for future vacancies, especially if 'lack of experience' or 'training' are issues.

Once you have addressed these matters, you may have exactly the list of attributes the company wants.

Staying positive

Not being offered a job you really wanted is disappointing, but remember that it is only a job. The right position is out there, and sooner rather than later, you will find it and have an offer on the table.

THE KEY IS TO STAY FOCUSED AND POSITIVE AS YOU LOOK FOR YOUR NEXT MOVE. THIS CAN BE ESPECIALLY DIFFICULT IF:

1 You are currently unemployed.

2 You are frustrated in your current position.

3 You dislike your boss/your colleagues/the company ethos.

4 Everyone around you seems to be finding a dream position.

WAYS TO STAY FOCUSED

■ **Network.** This is the single most effective way to locate a new position. Build up your contacts with others in your industry, develop new contacts in other industries you could possibly move into, increase your profile in any professional bodies, get in touch with people in your alumni association. The more people who know you are looking for a new position, the more likely you are to locate one.

■ **Read the trade journals.** Not only are these a good source of recruitment advertisements, but the news and features will keep you up to speed with developments, which will stand you in good stead for your next interview.

■ **Sign on with a recruitment consultant or an executive search company.** In general, as you climb higher up the ladder, fewer jobs are advertised.

■ **Take the initiative for your professional development.** Build new skills to add to your portfolio of marketable attributes. If you take continuing education courses in other fields, you will be doing firsthand detective work that may prove invaluable. And you will be in a great position to cultivate new contacts.

IMPROVING YOUR CURRENT POSITION

If you are frustrated where you are, have you said so? Sometimes managers do not realize that staff members need a fresh challenge. If you are due a performance review, make it a priority to say that you feel you could do more; there may be a project waiting in the wings that would suit you, while you continue to try to find a new position. It may also be the case that having a three- or six-month project to put on your CV is what will tip the balance at your next interview.

Your attitude makes a difference, so focus on what is good about your job – it is mentally challenging, you have met a deadline or exceeded a target – rather than on its frustrations.

TRAINING NEEDS

You probably know deep down that you are unlikely to make the next rung in your chosen career without further training, and the last interview pointed out this fact. If you need to do a course, now is the time to work out:

◼ When you can start

◼ How long it might take

◼ Whether you can do it full-time or part-time

◼ Whether you can identify benefits for your current employer (in which case they might pay, or at least give you paid study leave)

MOVING SIDEWAYS

Sometimes the best move is not necessarily upward. If you are very unhappy with your current position and are not getting past the interview process, assess whether a move to a different department or different part of the organization would help. This might:

■ Improve your CV

■ Heighten your motivation

■ Make you more relaxed at the next interview

■ Showcase your versatility

MOVING IN ANOTHER DIRECTION

You might consider a return to 'individual contributor' status. This may involve a reduction in salary, but the rewards of not managing others might prove worth it.

Career pathways

A broad sense of where you want to be, along with a receptive approach to opportunities that present themselves, means that most careers twist and turn along the way.

It is increasingly unusual for somebody to stay with a company for all of their career. The pace of change may mean you are likely to be faced with a need to rethink your career path several times during your working life. This may be forced on you by a technological change or changes in your own circumstances that require you to alter the way you work. This will require you to analyze the marketplace and look for the strategic movements that are taking place.

A sensible approach is to look for transferable skills – these are the skills that you identified before going to an interview that could be used in another sector of the workforce. Examples of transferable skills include communication, management and planning.

Your skills include the ability to apply knowledge and understanding of yourself and the labour market to individual decisions about career direction, allowing you to arrive at some conclusions on where you might be headed next. It involves a combination of self-analysis and acquisition of information from jobs and employers.

1 Where might your existing skills be best utilized?

2 Could you work for yourself?

3 Can you take business skills into the academic world, or vice versa?

4 Can you take life skills into business?

5 Where do you really want to be in two years?

Checklist: marketing strategies

The way you market and sell yourself is your foundation for effective career planning and management.

1 Know yourself.

2 Believe in yourself.

3 Improve your communication skills.

4 Treat change as a challenge and opportunity.

5 Make decisions – and if they are wrong, learn from them.

6 Build on your strengths.

7 Know what is happening now and predict what is likely in the future.

8 Make prospective employers an offer they can't refuse.

9 Know what people want and give them more.

10 Always look to the future.

Eliciting outside assistance

You have several options when it comes to utilizing others to find your next position for you.

CAREER COUNSELLORS

A career counsellor will not find a job or arrange interviews for you. Their role is to offer advice on where you might consider looking next, upgrade your CV and improve your interview skills.

A big part of what counsellors do is to help individuals identify career options and possibilities, based on a systematic process of assessment. Counsellors also assist clients in overcoming barriers to advancement and implementing a strategic job search campaign. Counsellors can charge large fees, but if you are committed to moving on, this can be worth the investment. Always ask for and check any references.

RECRUITMENT AGENCIES

Recruitment agencies match potential employees to vacancies. They will not get a job for you, that's up to you, but they will give advice on upgrading your CV and arrange interviews. An employer may pay:

■ On a contingency basis: that is, the employer pays if the shortlist of potential candidates the recruitment agency puts together leads to a successful hire.

■ On a retainer: that is, the seeking company pays whether or not a successful candidate is found by the recruitment agency.

Always read the contract with a recruitment agency carefully and get a copy of it for your own records.

If an agency is only paid for successful hires, you will only be put forward if you are already a good match. What you get out of such an arrangement is a chance to apply for a position that has not been advertised.

TEMPORARY RECRUITMENT AGENCIES

A temporary agency puts you on its books, finds you work and pays you for it. This kind of work is good in a lean spell, if you are looking to change direction or if you are unsure about where you want to go next in your career. If you are interested in a permanent position, you should state to the agency that you are interested in this type of assignment. Temp-to-hire conversions are possible.

Checklist: a lifelong process

Planning your career is a lifelong process. From the time you first define your career goals, you should be continually working out where you want to go next. Interviews are simply steps along the way. This checklist may help:

1 Define and then refine your career objectives.

2 Update your objectives regularly, at least as often as you update your CV.

3 Identify the resources you need to get you where you want to be: anything from a day seminar to a new degree.

4 Actively seek out job opportunities.

5 Choose a mentor or role model and learn from his or her style and achievements.

6 Take at least one positive from every interview.

7 Be a lifelong learner: constantly update skills and acquire new knowledge.

8 Be receptive to change and innovation.

9 Network (see pp. 224–225).

10 Accept that your values, skills and interests will change as your circumstances change.

CHECKLIST

Index